W9-ADZ-776

THE MARSHALL CAVENDISH
☆ ☆ ☆ ILLUSTRATED ☆ ☆ ☆
ENCYCLOPEDIA OF
WORLD WAR II

VOLUME 11

US140

THE MARSHALL CAVENDISH ☆ ☆ ☆ ILLUSTRATED ☆ ☆ ☆ ENCYCLOPEDIA OF WORLD WAR II

Based on the original text by
Lieutenant Colonel Eddy Bauer

CONSULTANT EDITOR

Brigadier General James L. Collins, Jr., U.S.A.

CHIEF OF MILITARY HISTORY,
DEPARTMENT OF THE ARMY

MARSHALL CAVENDISH CORPORATION/NEW YORK

CONTENTS

Editorial Director: Brian Innes
Editor-in-chief; Brigadier Peter Young, D.S.O., M.C., M.A.
Managing Editor: Richard Humble
Editor: Christopher Chant
Art Editor: Jim Bridge

Library of Congress Catalog No. 72-95429
Printed in Spain

CHAPTER 102
Allied problems, 1944

1944 saw the implementation of the political and military decisions taken as a result of the three inter-Allied conferences held at Quebec, Cairo, and Teheran. And so it seems appropriate here to discuss the solutions agreed on by Roosevelt and Churchill at Quebec in August 1943 and between these two statesmen, Chiang Kai-shek, and Stalin in Cairo and Teheran in November of that year.

Up till then, questions concerning the war itself had prevailed – and rightly so – at Allied meetings. But from the Quebec Conference onwards, the discussions ranged over a wider field. The victories of the British and Americans in the North Atlantic and in the Mediterranean, the steps taken by Mussolini's successor in Lisbon to get Italy out of the war, the Cassibile armistice, the fortunate outcome of the Battle of Kursk, the favourable progress of the Soviet offensive in the Ukraine, and finally the reversal of fortune in the Pacific, all inclined the four great powers, including China in the number, not to limit their discussions merely to finding solutions to the strategic problems of the moment.

Certainly, final arrangements still had to be settled between London and Washington in order to assure the success of Operation "Overlord", which at the moment was supplanting "Round-up". Likewise, operations against Japan would have to be intensified and the Indian Ocean and Burma theatres needed reactivating. In spite of American aid, the armies of Chiang Kai-shek had shown worrying signs of weakness the previous spring, and this disturbed President Roosevelt greatly. Churchill, however, cared less about the fate of China, but impatiently awaited the chance of wiping out the humiliation of Singapore and restoring the prestige of the Union Jack in that part of the world.

But nevertheless, even without counting chickens before they were hatched, it was time, if events were not to overwhelm the Allies, to get down to a serious examination of the future of Germany once the Third Reich had been invaded and forced into unconditional surrender. And this meant that attention would be given at the same time to the question of the countries of Central Europe and the Balkans which Hitler had subjugated or associated in his enterprises.

Furthermore, as soon as Japanese military power had been destroyed, it would be necessary to provide for the future of South-East Asia, which the common victory would free from Japanese occupation and exploitation. The least that can be said here is that Roosevelt's

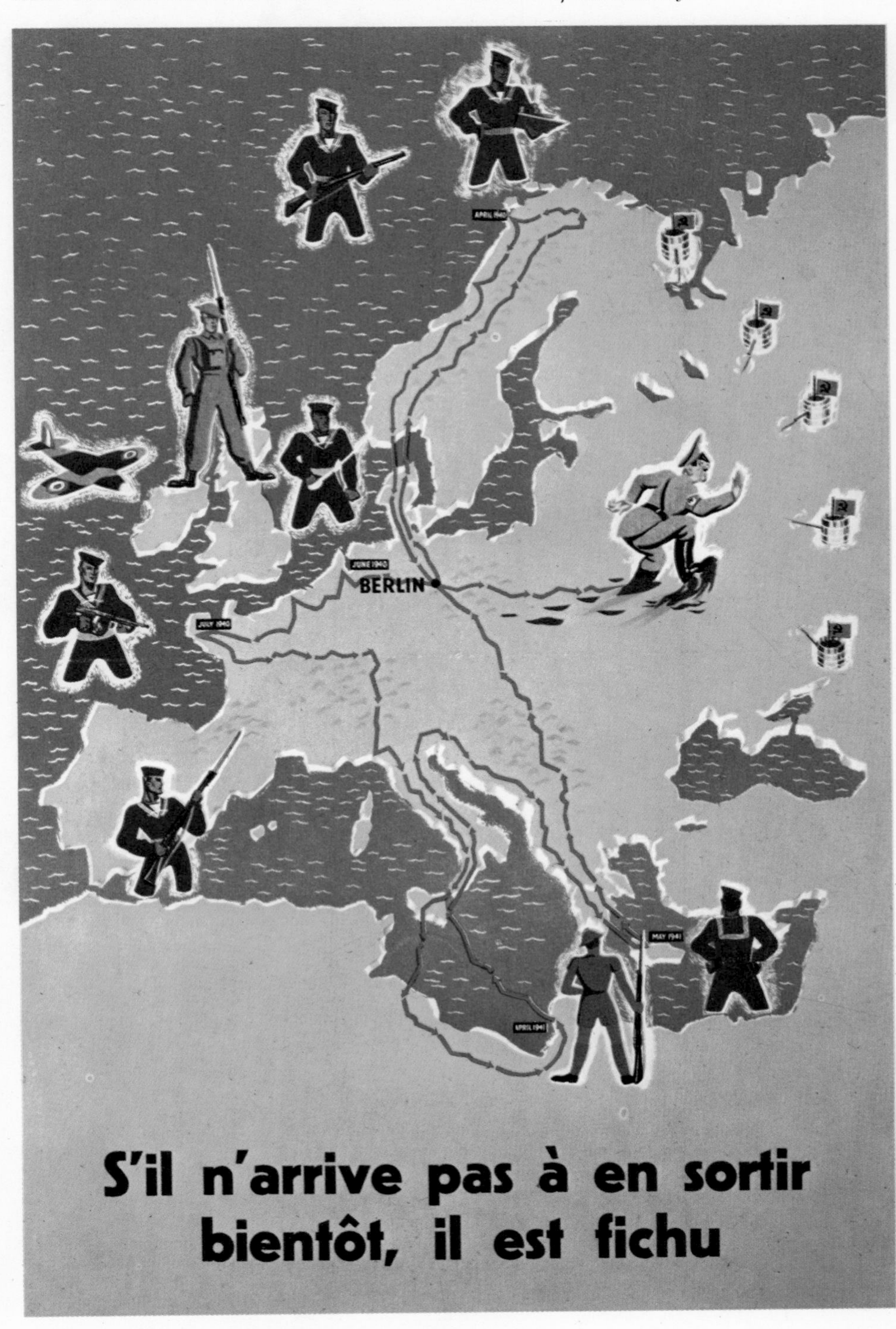

▽ *Caged in Europe, Hitler tries to break out of a cordon of Allied forces in this Free French poster. Though the Germans held most of Europe, their control was never complete as resistance movements could survive in cities as well as remote areas of the country.*

▷ *General Jan Smuts, C.-in-C. and Prime Minister of South Africa. During the war he became the valued friend and adviser of Churchill, and joined in meetings of the War Cabinet, as well as visiting South African troops in the field.*
▷▷ *Generalissimo Chiang Kai-shek. He was a symbol of resistance for the Allies in the Far East, having been at war with the Japanese since 1937. When he attended the Cairo Conference in 1943, it became in Roosevelt's words "Chiang's conference".*

ideas on the best way to go about this were quite different from those of Churchill.

Finally, once peace had been re-established all over the globe, it would be necessary to unite all countries under the United Nations, an idea which sprang from the Atlantic Charter. The United Nations would be a new world organisation, more efficient than the old League of Nations in maintaining peace, promoting libertarian government, and checking any return to the spirit of aggression and conquest wherever it might appear.

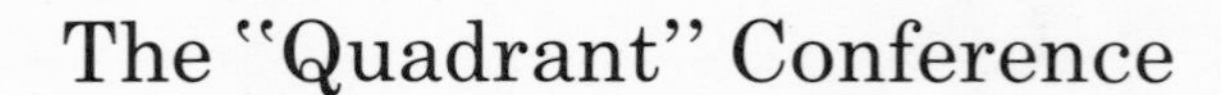

The "Quadrant" Conference

Not all these questions were touched on during the "Quadrant" Conference, which lasted from August 19 to August 24, 1943. It was held in Quebec and present were the President of the United States, the British Prime Minister, and their civil and military staffs. Those questions which went beyond the limits of war strategy required the presence of Joseph Stalin and Chiang Kai-shek and, on these subjects, the White House had no wish to maintain a "special relationship", as it would be called today, with 10 Downing Street.

On the advice of the Combined Chiefs-of-Staff, the principle of Operation "Overlord" was definitely adopted. It would be launched across the Channel on or about May 1, 1944. The report stated:

"This operation will be the primary United States–British ground and air effort against the Axis in Europe. (Target date, May 1, 1944.) After securing adequate Channel ports, exploitation will be directed towards securing areas that will facilitate both ground and air operations against the enemy. Following the establishment of strong Allied forces in France, operations designed to strike at the heart of Germany and to destroy her military forces will be undertaken."

Had Winston Churchill and Sir Alan

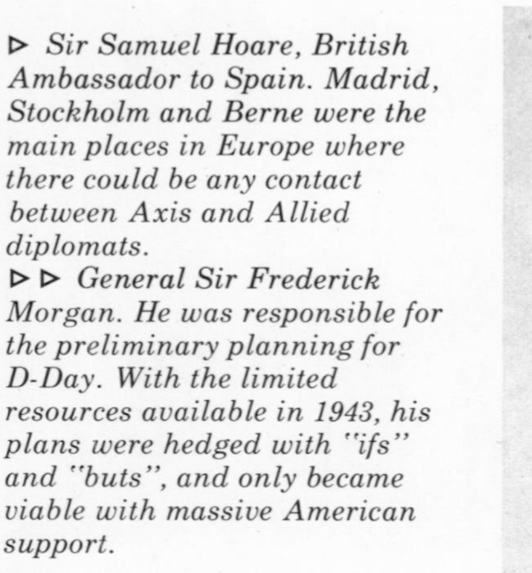

▷ *Sir Samuel Hoare, British Ambassador to Spain. Madrid, Stockholm and Berne were the main places in Europe where there could be any contact between Axis and Allied diplomats.*
▷▷ *General Sir Frederick Morgan. He was responsible for the preliminary planning for D-Day. With the limited resources available in 1943, his plans were hedged with "ifs" and "buts", and only became viable with massive American support.*

◁◁ *Averell Harriman, appointed U.S. Ambassador to Moscow in 1943. He had led missions to Britain and the U.S.S.R. to negotiate Lend-Lease terms. In Moscow he was granted an unprecedented monthly interview with Stalin to discuss a wide range of topics involved in Russo-American co-operation.*
◁ *General Bissel, head of the United States Information Services, who suppressed the report by Colonel van Vliet of the U.S. Army, who claimed the Russians were responsible for the Katyn massacre.*

Brooke accepted the principle of a Second Front in Western Europe without reservations? Within the Pentagon and in the President's immediate circle, the sincerity of their agreement was doubted. However, the smallest doubt about Churchill's intentions was swept away by the cable which the British premier addressed to his friend Smuts. The South African Prime Minister had said that in his opinion the Normandy landings should be put off in order not to run short of the resources which would allow the Allies to exploit their Mediterranean successes in Italy and in the Balkan peninsula. Churchill replied:

"There can be no question whatever of breaking arrangements we have made with the United States for 'Overlord' . . . I hope you will realise that British loyalty to 'Overlord' is keystone of arch of Anglo-American co-operation. Personally I think enough forces exist for both hands to be played, and I believe this to be the right strategy."

As it happened, the strategy that Churchill talks about in this cable would be seen to be less "right" than he imagined when he was writing, but the text which he quotes here demonstrates the firmness with which he supported the idea of a Second Front. The Chief of the Imperial General Staff had also given up his suspicions about it.

American hegemony

Brooke thus experienced a bitter disappointment when he learned that Churchill and Roosevelt had agreed to put an American over his head as supreme commander of "Overlord".

"The end of a gloomy and unpleasant day," Brooke noted on August 15. Three years later, describing the way Churchill told him about the decision, he wrote ". . . As Winston spoke all that scenery was swamped by a dark cloud of despair. I had voluntarily given up the opportunity of taking over the North African Com-

◁◁ *Lord Louis Mountbatten. He became Supreme Allied Commander, S.E. Asia in October 1943 after directing Combined Operations. The Dieppe raid laid the foundations for much of the "Overlord" operation, and though it seemed a costly failure General Morgan said "Without Dieppe 'Overlord' would have proved impossible."*
◁ *Harry Hopkins, close confidant and adviser of President Roosevelt. Churchill said of him he was "the most faithful and perfect channel of communications."*

▵ *One for the camera: the Royal Canadian Mounted Police detachment at Quebec is inspected as a press photographer gets his picture.*
▹ *Quebec, August 1943.* Seated left to right, *Mackenzie King, Prime Minister of Canada; Roosevelt, Churchill;* standing: *Brooke, King, Dill, Marshall, and Pound.*

mand before El Alamein and recommended that Alexander should be appointed instead. I had done so . . . because I felt at that time I could probably serve a more useful purpose by remaining with Winston. But now when the strategy of the war had been guided to the final stage–the stage when the real triumph of victory was to be gathered–I felt no longer necessarily tied to Winston and free to assume this Supreme Command which he had already promised me on three separate occasions. It was a crushing blow to hear from him he was now handing over this appointment to the Americans, and had in exchange received the agreement of the President to Mountbatten's appointment as Supreme Commander for South-East Asia. Not for one moment did he realise what this meant to me. He offered no sympathy, no regrets at having to change his mind, and dealt with the matter as if it were one of minor importance."

Nevertheless, neither of the two men had liked the plans that he had given up. In fact the "C.O.S.S.A.C." plan, drawn up by an Anglo-American committee under the leadership of the British Lieutenant-General F. E. Morgan, Chief-of-Staff Supreme Allied Commander, no longer risked difficulty in planning to disembark troops between Deauville and Calais. By now it was thinking in terms of the first bridgehead being established on the Calvados coast which was less steep, fortified, and garrisoned than the coasts of upper Normandy and Picardy. Furthermore, its beaches were quite well protected against the south-westerly winds.

Another important point was that the ingenuity of Lord Louis Mountbatten and Captain Hughes-Hallett had made it possible to begin the construction of prefabricated harbours in Great Britain, as a result of which the supplying of troops fighting in lower Normandy could be maintained without having to wait for Cherbourg to be captured. Protected from the open sea by a breakwater made from enormous concrete blocks ("Phoenix") and intentionally scuttled ships ("Gooseberries"), these artificial harbours, called "Mulberries" in order to camouflage their existence, would have to be equipped with articulated jetties whose piers would rise and fall with the tide. A million tons of steel and cement went into their construction.

With these new aspects of the question, it can easily be understood that the Prime Minister and the Chief of the Imperial General Staff looked forward optimistically to the results of "Overlord" in 1944, while "Round-up" had seemed extremely hazardous to them at the close of September 1943, and to carry intolerable risks in the autumn of 1942.

In fact, the results showed that they were right. Nevertheless, while receiving Churchill in his fine family home of Hyde Park, when the Anglo-American Combined Chiefs-of-Staff Committee was getting down to work at Quebec, President Roosevelt was confronted by a memorandum from Secretary of War Henry Stimson, demanding that General Marshall be given command of "Overlord", basing his insistence on the following:

"We cannot now rationally hope to be able to cross the Channel and come to grips with our German enemy under a British commander. His Prime Minister and his Chief of the Imperial Staff are frankly at variance with such a proposal. The shadows of Passchendaele and Dunquerque still hang too heavily over the imagination of these leaders of his Government. Though they have rendered lip-service to the operation, their hearts are not in it and it will require more independence, more faith, and more vigour than it is reasonable to expect we can find

Previous page: *Mackenzie King, host to three illustrious guests. With Churchill and Roosevelt is Field-Marshal Sir John Dill, British military representative in the U.S.A. The Quebec conference laid down the principle of an invasion of Europe in summer 1944, provided that the Germans would be unable to oppose the landing with more than 12 mobile divisions and that their air fighter strength in the West should have been considerably diminished.*

in any British commander . . ."

The Secretary for War went on to stress the "fundamental difference" in approach which was still apparent between the two Allied staffs. The British still believed in wearing-down operations and scattering the invasion force between Northern Italy, the Balkans, Greece and the Mediterranean, Stimson wrote: "None of these methods of pinprick warfare can be counted on by us to fool Stalin into the belief that we have kept that pledge."

Churchill makes no reference in his memoirs to this memorandum, which mirrored the point of view of the American military leaders. President Roosevelt accepted their conclusions and used other arguments to persuade his guest that Alan Brooke should be replaced by Marshall as C.-in-C. of "Overlord". What he argued, in fact, was that since two-thirds of the forces in the enterprise were to be American, it was logical that an American should command them.

A new theatre is born

Churchill agreed with this argument and gave in hoping for a considerable reciprocal advantage. Here he was mistaken.

Certainly he managed to obtain the establishment of a new theatre of war in South-East Asia and to have the command given to Lord Louis Mountbatten, with whose capability he was infatuated and whom he had taken with him to Quebec. But he was not at all successful when he put forward the idea of an amphibious operation, "Culverin", whose object was to occupy the Japanese-held north-west part of the island of Sumatra. Sir Alan Brooke thought this plan was a mirage, as he explains in his autobiography:

"It was not a suitable base for further operations against Malaya, but I could not get any definite reply from him as to what he hoped to accomplish from there. When I drew his attention to the fact that when he put his left foot down he should know where the right foot was going to, he shook his fist in my face, saying, 'I do not want any of your long-term projects. They cripple initiative!' I agreed that they did hamper initiative, but told him that I could not look upon knowing where our next step was going as constituting a long-term project. I told him he must know where he was going, to which he replied that he did not want to know."

The Americans, for their part, believed that the Allied effort in this sector of the Pacific should aim at restoring with China a link more effective than the airlift which, since the previous spring, had linked the supply bases in India with Chunking over the Himalayas, or the Ledo route which had just been improved. This meant an offensive in Burma and the recapture of only the Andaman Islands in the Indian Ocean.

The Mediterranean, a thorny problem

But it was on the question of the strategy to be adopted in the Mediterranean that the clash between the two English-speaking allies was sharpest. On this point, General Sir Alan Brooke and his colleagues were solidly behind Churchill.

According to the well-informed testimony of Admiral William D. Leahy, the American President's Chief-of-Staff, the crisis reached flashpoint on August 14. On that day he noted:

"General Marshall was very positive in his attitude against a Mediterranean commitment. Admiral King was determined not to have a single additional warship so badly needed in the Pacific operations diverted to any extra operations in that area so favoured by our British allies. British insistence on expanding the Italian operations provoked King to very undiplomatic language, to use a mild term."

What had been the straw to break the camel's back and had provoked the irascible Admiral beyond measure was Brooke's question whether the double push planned for the Pacific could not be scaled down to a single line of thrust.

As can be seen, the two delegations clashed more than anything else on the question of the distribution of amphibious vessels and landing-craft. On June 6, 1944 King, who had defended his ships with the obstinacy of a dog guarding a bone, had under his own and MacArthur's command 3,866 of these craft against the 3,696 taking part in Operation "Overlord", and 1,037 operating in the Mediterranean. If the share-out of these vessels caused such tension at this date in inter-Allied meetings, what would have been the situation if the Allies had kept to their original timetable, which had stipulated a landing n September 1943? A large proportion of the ships were not even in service until 1944.

Italy and the Balkans: secondary fronts?

There remains one more point to be considered in this split between the British and the Americans. Is it true, as Stimson and Marshall thought, that both Churchill and Brooke were inclined to fritter away the forces of the English-speaking alliance in operations outside the principal ones? This brings up the question of whether, by August 15, Italy and the Balkans should be considered as secondary sectors. Doubtless they could, against the background of the entire war, but not at all in the circumstances of the moment, because only in the Mediterranean could the Western Allies attack the enemy, now that "Overlord" had been put off till May 1, 1944. Meanwhile, should Hitler be left a free hand? This was the question that occasioned Field-Marshal Smuts' cable to Churchill previously mentioned.

Hitler was, in fact, reassured about the Allies' intentions in the Mediterranean and decided to transfer three armoured divisions to O.K.H. These were the 1st Panzer Division, which had been sent to garrison the Peloponnese, and the 24th Panzer Division, and the *"Leibstandarte" Panzergrenadier* Division of the *Waffen* S.S., which formed Field-Marshal Rommel's strategic reserve in northern Italy. All three were attached to Army Group "South" and took part in the counter-offensive which enabled Field-Marshal von Manstein temporarily to recapture Zhitomir. In this particular case, then, it is evident that the restrictions imposed on Mediterranean operations by the Combined Chiefs-of-Staff Committee were not very helpful to the Red Army in its struggle with the Wehrmacht.

The report adopted by the Chiefs-of-Staff on August 19 was quite definite on the matter.

"Where there is a shortage of resources available resources will be distributed and employed with the main object of ensuring the success of 'Overlord'. Operations in the Mediterranean theatre will be carried out with the forces allotted at 'Trident' [the previous Conference at Washington in May], except in so far as these may be varied by decision of the Combined Chiefs-of-Staff."

For practical purposes, once these principles had been laid down, Allied objectives in this sector of the war were limited to the conquest of Sardinia, Corsica, and southern Italy. But it was already understood that once the Allied 15th Army Group had crossed the Tiber, it would have to give up some of its forces to the 6th Army Group charged with a new operation, "Anvil", a landing in the south of France, to combine with the hammer blow of "Overlord".

"At Quebec the decision was made," according to Robert Sherwood, "to supplement the Normandy invasion with landings by American and newly armed French forces in the Toulon-Marseilles area of Southern France. This was an operation–it was known first as ANVIL and later as DRAGOON–against which Churchill fought implacably until within a few days of its accomplishment on August 15, 1944, whereupon he turned up aboard a British destroyer in the Mediterranean and, with apparent exultation, waved the victory sign to the astonished troops as they headed for the Riviera beaches."

△ *Indispensable companions to any great man, the wives of the three political leaders at Quebec. Their presence prompted a social round, which Brooke, for one, did not approve. "These continual lunches, dinners and cocktail parties were a serious interruption to our work. When occupied with continuous conferences, time is required to collect one's thoughts, read papers and write notes."*

Between the German invasion of Russia in June 1941 and the Allied invasion of Italy in September 1943, the burden of the Allied war effort on the continent of Europe fell squarely on the shoulders of the Russian soldier. Rising above the murderous defeats of the first phase of *"Barbarossa"* in June–December 1941, the Red Army not only survived as a fighting entity but immediately proved itself to be the foremost instrument of armed resistance to Germany.

One of the greatest mistakes Hitler ever made was to underestimate the grass-root patriotism of the Russian soldier. Even in the weeks of apparent national collapse in 1941, the steadfastness of the Russian troops appalled the men of the Wehrmacht. Abominably led, thrown into the battle in driblets, the Red Army's infantry charged the German machine guns head-on with linked arms, cheering *"Za rodinu, za Stalina"* ("For the motherland, for Stalin") until the sickened German gunners could hardly bring themselves to fire another shot.

If it was magnificent it was certainly not war, and yet within months the Red Army had gone over to the offensive and was threatening to annihilate the German Army Group "Centre". Only the self-destructive, wide-front strategy insisted on by Stalin, and the slap-dash tactics used during the offensive, robbed the Red Army of victory.

When the Germans attacked again in the summer of 1942 they soon found how much the Red Army had learned since its mauling in 1941. As Army Group "South" drove east to the Volga and south to the Caucasus, the Russians pulled back, refusing to get trapped in vast pockets and conserving their superiority in manpower. And at Stalingrad the incredible endurance and fighting spirit of the Russian soldier were

"HONOUR TO THE RED ARMY!"

1. *A Russian assault group moves into position in a workers' settlement in the northern Caucasus.*
2. *A Cossack patrol crosses the Don. Cavalry was used until the end of the war for reconnaissance and as mounted infantry.*
3. *An 82-mm mortar in action; used against troops in wooded areas, mortar bombs would burst amongst the branches giving an air burst effect.*
4. *Soviet infantry advance into the misty shadows of a Russian wood.*

3

. With one man on guard with
he DP light machine gun, a
group of Red soldiers take a
meal break. Note the sub-machine
guns and rifle within easy
each.
. The Morozov Cossack
avalry division attacks on the
Voronezh front.
. Russian soldiers bringing a
mortar into action under fire.
. A Soviet 76-mm gun in
position to cover a bridge.
. Czech troops fighting on the
Eastern front with an ambulance
presented by the Czech
community of Canada.

proved for all time in the vicious hand-to-hand fighting in the shattered ruins of the city.

The Red Army's successes at winter fighting were not caused by the immunity of the Russian soldier to cold, but were the result of sensible equipment. Nothing, however, can detract from the fact that right from the beginning of the war in Russia the men of the Red Army earned themselves a reputation for unbelievable toughness, which impressed even the veteran soldiers of the Wehrmacht.

Even when the Red Army went over to the offensive its losses remained high, owing to the sledgehammer tactics of the front commanders. Yet the Russian soldier was willing to endure this as well. All in all he certainly deserved the propaganda salute of "Honour to the Red Army!"

HOLLANDER
FINNEN
LITTAUER
LEINE STAATEN
EUROPAS

◁ *German comment on Russian ambitions. A gross Soviet soldier comments "You can see how happy these people are that you've abandoned to be liberated by me". From the pot marked "Little European States", Lithuania, Finland, and Holland peer in apprehension.*
△ *A German view of the Italian armistice. "Away with dregs" says the cartoon of the Nazi brush cleaning the Italian boot.*
▷ △ *"A new invention of the point blank shooting specialist: This is how we'll prepare the table for the next conference" says a cheerful Stalin in this cartoon from* Kladderadatsch *of Berlin.*
▷ *With the prospect of ultimate victory* The Rand Daily Mail *could afford to be facetious, but by the end of the War, Germany's Balkan allies would have turned against her.*

CHAPTER 103

KATYN: the burden of guilt

▷ *"Man Eater"–the original of this Russian cartoon was presented to Lord Beaverbrook by Stalin. It is typical of the savage Russian style, which served to whip up hatred in its readers, rather than the Western ones that ridiculed the Axis, making them objects of fun.*

As previously explained, the military situation, as it appeared at the time of the "Quadrant" Conference, was sufficiently hopeful to make the British and the Americans begin to think of the future of the European continent and its balance of power after German military might, which had changed the entire pre-war picture, had been reduced to dust and ashes.

There are two documents to be taken into account in this question. One comes from the pen of a senior American officer whom Robert E. Sherwood, editing the Harry Hopkins papers, could not identify. The other comes from a letter that Churchill sent to Field-Marshal Smuts personally on September 5, 1943.

When Harry Hopkins went to Quebec, he carried with him a note entitled "The Russian position", in which the anonymous American officer gave his views concerning post-war prospects in Europe and the chances of obtaining the help of Russia in the struggle against Japan:

"Russia's post-war position in Europe will be a dominant one. With Germany crushed, there is no power in Europe to oppose her tremendous military forces. It is true that Great Britain is building up a position in the Mediterranean *vis-à-vis* Russia that she may find useful in balancing power in Europe. However, even here she may not be able to oppose Russia unless she is otherwise supported.

"The conclusions from the foregoing are obvious. Since Russia is the decisive factor in the war, she must be given every assistance and every effort must be made to obtain her friendship. Likewise, since without question she will dominate Europe on the defeat of the Axis, it is even more essential to develop and maintain the most friendly relations with Russia.

"Finally, the most important factor the United States has to consider in relation to Russia is the prosecution of the war in Pacific. With Russia as an ally in the war against Japan, the war can be terminated in less time and at less expense in life and resources than if the reverse were the case. Should the war in the Pacific have to be carried on with an unfriendly or negative attitude on the part of Russia, the difficulties will be immeasurably increased and the operations might become abortive."

Churchill saw things in much the same light. His old South African friend, disappointed by the results of the Quebec Conference, which slowed down the war in the Mediterranean, cabled him on September 3:

"To the ordinary man it must appear that it is Russia who is winning the war. If this impression continues what will be our post-war world position compared with that of Russia? A tremendous shift in our world status may follow, and will leave Russia the diplomatic master of the world. This is both unnecessary and undesirable, and would have especially bad reactions for the British Commonwealth. Unless we emerge from the war on terms of equality our position will be both uncomfortable and dangerous."

Two days later, Churchill replied "after profound reflection", in a cable outlining eight points. Only the sixth is quoted here because it deals in particular with the question under discussion:

"I think it inevitable that Russia will be the greatest land Power in the world after this war, which will have rid her of two military Powers, Japan and Germany, who in our lifetime have inflicted upon her such heavy defeats. I hope however that the 'fraternal association' of the British Commonwealth and the United States, together with sea- and air-power, may put us on good terms and in a friendly balance with Russia at least for the period of rebuilding. Farther than that I cannot see with mortal eye, and I am not as yet fully informed about the celestial telescopes."

Anti-Russian consensus

So, it is evident that neither the anonymous American officer's memorandum nor the man responsible for British policy were fundamentally opposed to the opinions expressed on February 21, 1943 by General Franco in his letter to Sir Samuel Hoare, at the time British Ambassador in Madrid, on the consequence of the military collapse of the Third Reich. But, in contrast to the report entitled *The*

France
Rumania
Poland
Greece
Belgium
Jugoslavia

∇ *The horrifying extent of the Katyn massacre: an aerial view of the bodies, packed in rows like dried fish.*
▷ *The investigation begins. One of the bodies is uncovered under the supervision of Professor Orsōs from the University of Budapest, the Hungarian delegate on the European commission invited by the Germans to visit the Katyn site.*

position of Russia, Churchill could not so easily accept the upsetting of the balance of power, and took some care to think about easing its most unpleasant consequences. So, in his opinion, after the war it would not be a good policy to loosen the Anglo-American ties which would have helped to win it. On September 6, with this in mind, he spoke to the staff and students of Harvard University, which had just conferred on him an honorary doctorate. He recalled the linguistic, literary, and legal heritage common to the two English-speaking democracies and, speaking beyond his immediate audience, exhorted Great Britain and the United States to strengthen their common purpose even more. In particular, he expressed the wish that the "marvellous" system of the Combined Chiefs-of-Staff Committee would not wind up, once the last shot had been fired.

"Now in my opinion it would be a most foolish and improvident act on the part of our two Governments, or either of them, to break up this smooth-running and immensely powerful machinery the moment the war is over. For our own safety, as well as for the security of the rest of the world, we are bound to keep it working and in running order after the war–probably for a good many years, not only until we have set up some world arrangement to keep the peace, but until we know that it is an arrangement which will really give us that protection we must have from danger and aggression, a protection we have already to seek across two vast world wars."

But President Roosevelt acted on the advice of Harry Hopkins and had no intention of following Churchill's plans. This would mean engaging the United States in a "special relationship" with Great Britain after the war. And so, in his memoirs, Churchill concludes, speaking of the rejection of his suggestion: "Alas, folly has already prevailed!"

Stalin's ill-will

The word "folly" was perhaps an over-exaggeration because Roosevelt and Hopkins did not possess, any more than did Churchill, a crystal ball which would give them some insight into the murky future of the world.

All the same, just like Churchill, Roosevelt had on file a large bundle of letters sent to him by Stalin, beginning on the date when Hitler's attack had destroyed the German-Soviet Non-Aggression Pact. The least that can be said is that neither in the style nor the content of these letters was there any sign which might allow any optimism for the future, even though when he wrote to the White House, Stalin took care to express himself more tactfully than when he wrote to Churchill.

Reading this correspondence Stalin's tone is seen to be distinctly arrogant and sarcastic, with hostile accusation against his allies, statements which are risky to say the least, an obstinate refusal to take any account of the opinions of others, a completely unconcealed expression of the most unpleasant suspicions, and an insatiable desire for revenge, sharpened by each concession or gift made by his Western partners.

From this time on, it was becoming abundantly clear that post-war relations between the Allies and peaceful collaboration between Moscow, London, and Washington would tend to be difficult, even supposing that the two English-

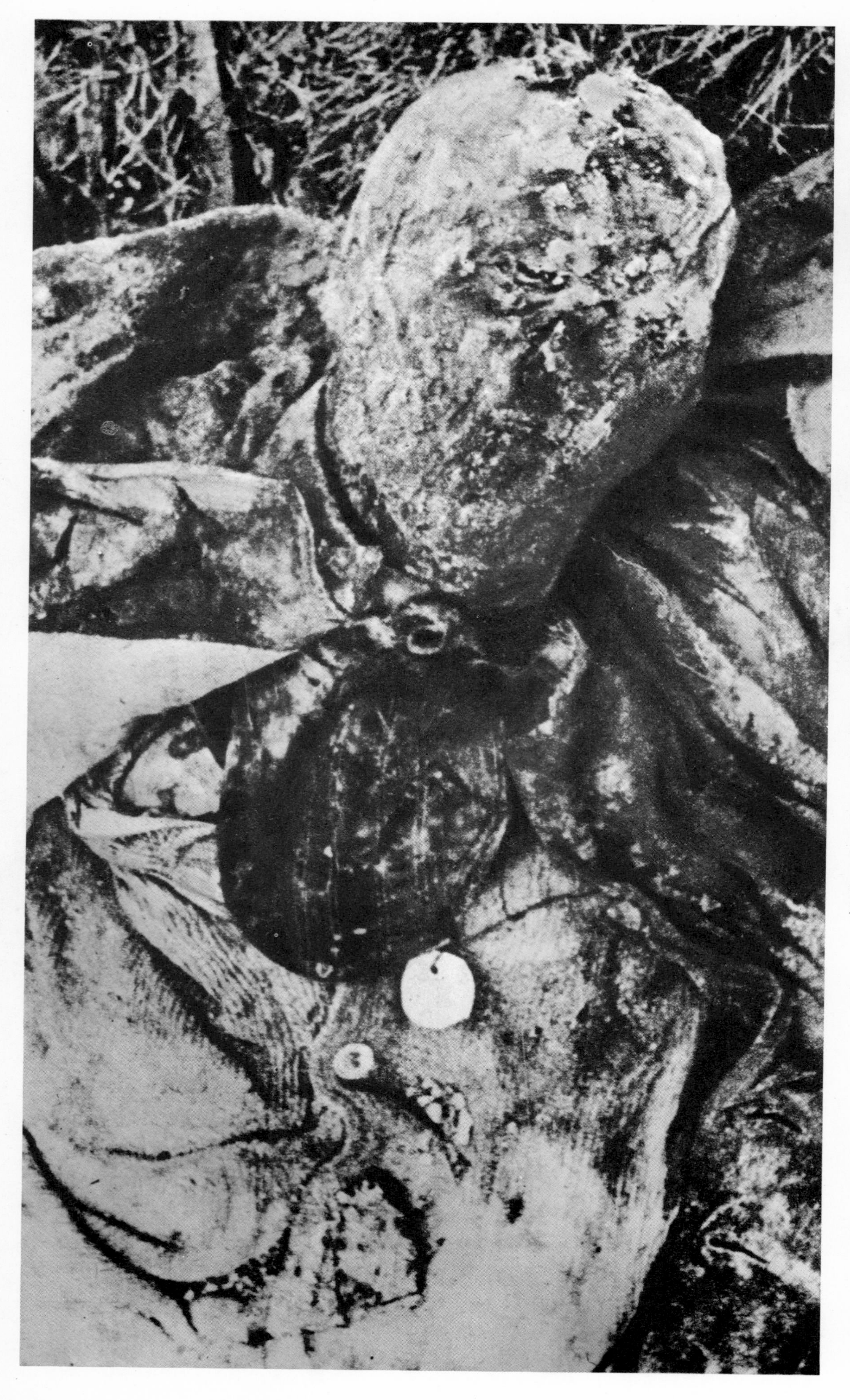

◁ *The body of a chaplain, identified as Jan Leon Zielkowski, still wearing his clerical bands.*
△ *The excavations revealed how the bodies were packed in parallel, stacked rows.*

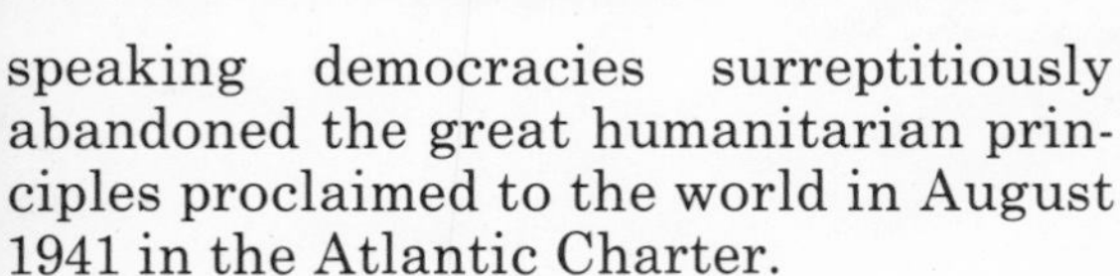

speaking democracies surreptitiously abandoned the great humanitarian principles proclaimed to the world in August 1941 in the Atlantic Charter.

Massacre at Katyn

At this point, should the ghastly charnel-house of Katyn be recalled? Here, six miles west of Smolensk, on April 13, 1943 the Germans found piled up 12 deep, the mummified bodies of 4,143 Polish officers, all felled by pistol shots in the back of the neck. It has been maintained that when the British and Americans learned of this example of Stalinist ferocity, they should have taken clear warning and had their eyes fully opened to the real nature of Soviet domination. Examination of the facts and the evidence require some modification of this opinion, however.

In fact, at the time neither Churchill nor Roosevelt had a complete dossier on the massacre which would clarify where the responsibility for Katyn lay. This would come out in 1946 at the international trial in Nuremberg and would be completed in 1952, when a House of Representatives' Committee would carry out an investigation.

Certainly neither one nor the other believed the emphatic statements of Stalin in the least. He told them on April 21, 1943, that Moscow was breaking off relations with the Polish Government-in-Exile. The terms used merit quotation:

"The fact that the anti-Soviet campaign has been started simultaneously in the German and Polish press and follows identical lines is indubitable evidence of contact and collusion between Hitler – the Allies' enemy – and the Sikorski Government in this hostile campaign.

"At a time when the peoples of the Soviet Union are shedding their blood in a grim struggle against Hitler's Germany and bending their energies to defeat the common foe of freedom-loving democratic countries, the Sikorski Government is striking a treacherous blow at the Soviet Union to help Hitler's tyranny."

It seems likely that Churchill never

△ *Found in the winter clothing of Chaplain Zielkowski: a breviary and a miniature altar and rosary, made in the camp at Kozielsk in 1940.*
Overleaf: *The biggest of the seven mass graves at Katyn was found to contain 2,500 bodies to a row, stacked in five layers.*

Le document de Katyn

▷ *The international committee at work, examining the personal effects found on the bodies.*

▽ *Professor Palmieri of Naples dissects a skull. He found that three bullets had been fired into the nape of the neck.*

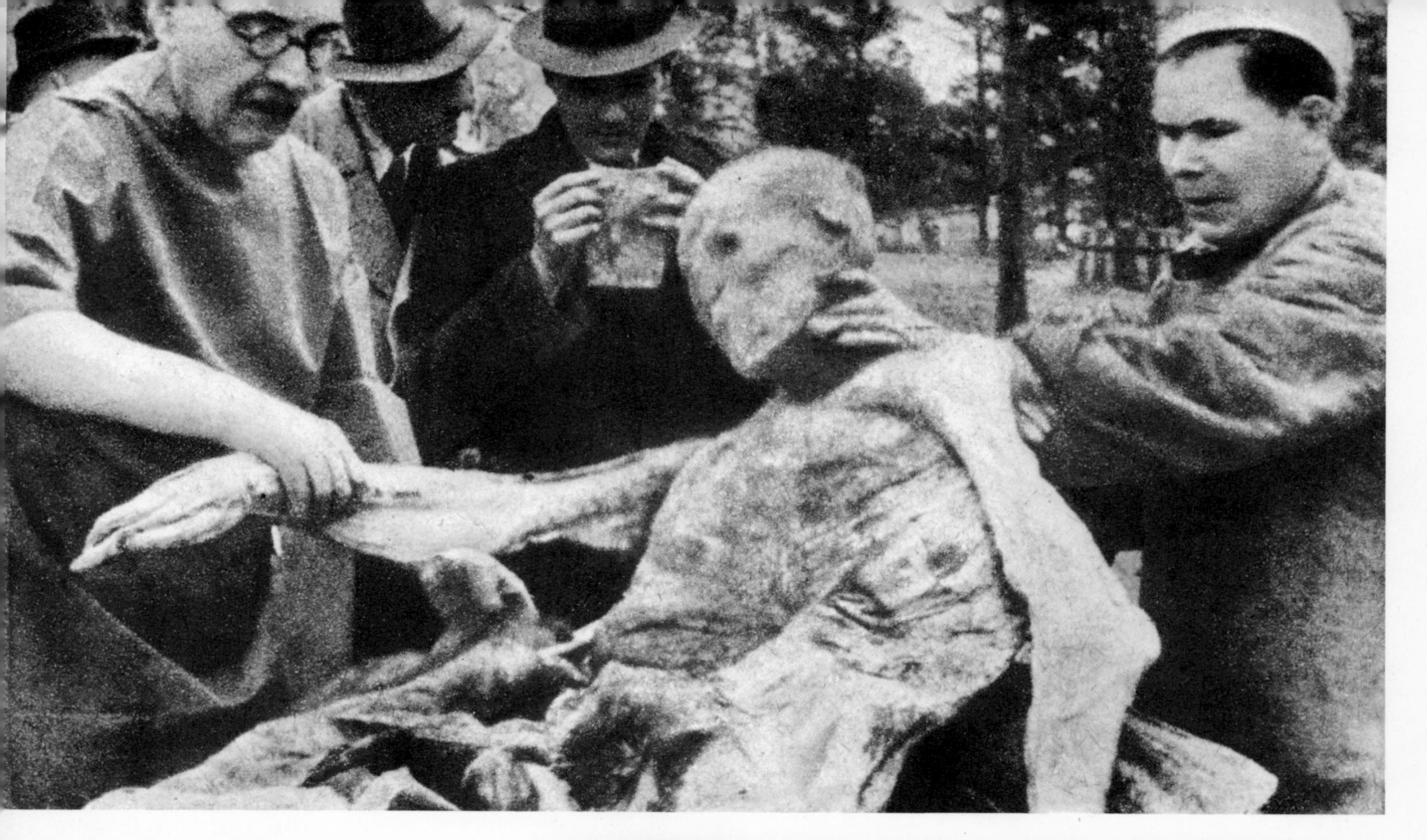

believed the Moscow version of the facts, which blamed the mass murder on the Germans. Perhaps it was the indignation caused by his conclusions on the massacre that was one of the motives which caused him to change his mind on the chances of co-operation between the Stalinist East and the Democratic West. But in the final analysis it had no influence on Anglo-American discussions.

President Roosevelt was the arbiter of the situation, and the many reports which arrived on his desk from the most reliable sources concerning the crimes perpetrated by the Nazis in most of the occupied countries led him to lay the massacre of the Polish officers at their door. Furthermore, perhaps his opinions were confirmed by a report on the massacre sent to him by Averell Harriman, his Ambassador in Moscow, on January 25, 1944, after the Red Army had retaken Smolensk.

On January 15, British and American press correspondents stationed in Moscow had travelled to Katyn to find out for themselves the conclusions reached by the committee appointed by the Soviet Government to clarify this frightful mystery and to hear some witnesses. The American Ambassador was permitted to send his daughter as one of his aides and, on the basis of her information, he formed his opinion. The prudence and intentional vagueness with which he expressed himself is noteworthy:

"None of the members of the group", he wrote to the State Department, "was qualified to judge the scientific evidence deduced by the autopsies carried out in their presence. They were not allowed to make personal enquiries but they could address definite questions to certain witnesses with whom they were confronted.

"The correspondents made reports on what they had seen without expressing any personal opinion but for some reason the censor withheld their report. The proofs and evidence are not very conclusive but Kathleen [his daughter] and the representative of the Embassy believe that the massacre was probably committed by the Germans."

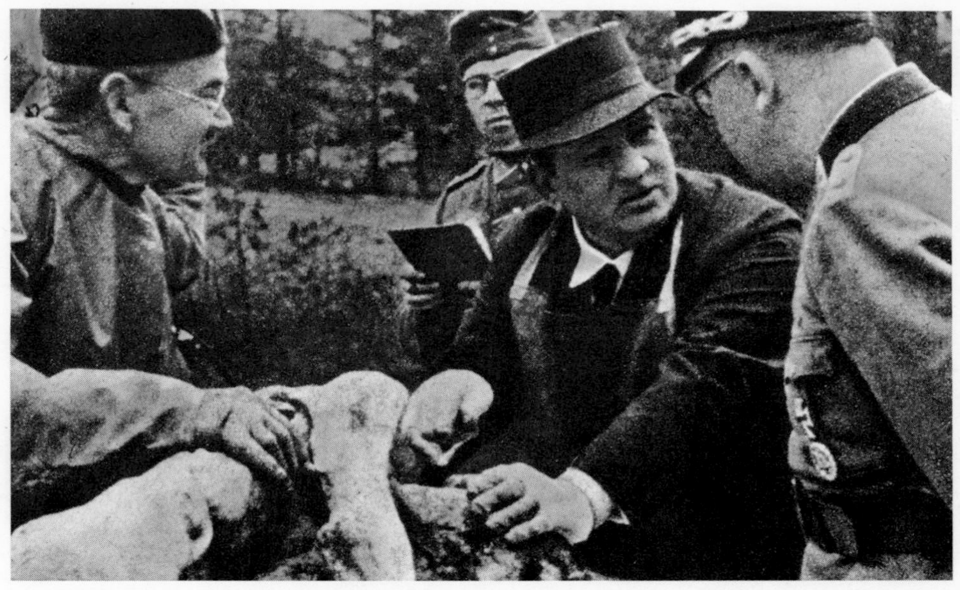

△△ A body is carefully stripped of its clothing. Professor Hajek of Prague examines documents found in the pockets.
△ Professor Milosavic of Zagreb tells Professor Buhtz, superintendent of the excavations, of his findings: death by shooting in the neck.

This was followed by factual appendices supporting this opinion, assembled by Miss Harriman. She, however, recognised frankly and without restraint that they were not very consistent when, as Mrs. Mortimer, she gave evidence on November 12, 1952 before the Investigating Committee of the House of Representatives.

It has also been said that, towards the end of his life, Roosevelt no longer believed that the Katyn massacre had been perpetrated by the Germans. Nevertheless, for evident reasons, he was no more able than Churchill to make a public declaration on the matter.

Soviet responsibilities

However, the historian of today must note that Katyn was introduced, during the summer of 1945, into the charges preferred against the German leaders accused of war crimes before the Nuremberg International Military Tribunal, and that this was done at the request of the Soviet prosecutor. Furthermore, after long discussions, all the zeal of Colonels Pokrovsky and Smirnov could not establish conclusive proof, and the charge of the murder of 11,000 Polish officers was not even mentioned in the Tribunal's verdict on the condemned men.

And so it is valid to conclude that the Soviet accusation did not risk trying to contradict the report which had been signed by 12 forensic experts on April 30, 1943. These latter had been invited to Berlin to visit the charnel-house at Katyn and had been authorised to conduct post-mortems freely on whichever bodies they chose. With the exception of Professor Naville of the University of Geneva, they all belonged to occupied or German satellite countries. Yet, with the exception of a Bulgarian, later acquitted after a pitiful self-accusation before a Sofia court, and a Czech, none of the 12 signatories agreed to go back on the declaration he had made in 1943.

In spite of the accusations made against him by a Communist deputy from Geneva, Professor Naville confirmed his evidence in September 1946, and was completely exonerated by the cantonal authorities of the suspicions that Moscow had tried to throw on his scientific reputation and professional probity. In 1952, Dr. Milosavić, once Director of the Institute of

Criminology and Forensic Medicine of Zagreb, Professor Palmieri of the University of Naples, and Dr. Tramsen, Head of Medical Services of the Royal Danish Navy, deported for acts of resistance by the Gestapo in 1944, maintained their statements before the American Committee of Enquiry, as did Professor Orsōs, of the University of Budapest.

After having examined the bodies, their clothing and the documents found on them, they came to the unanimous conclusion that the crime of Katyn could not be dated later than the beginning of spring 1940. The Russians, on the other hand, claim that the massacre had been perpetrated during August 1941, that is just after the battle in which the Germans overran the entire Smolensk region.

The controversy stifled

These separate opinions, from Europe and from America, are confirmed absolutely independently by the evidence of Colonel van Vliet of the United States Army, in a report dated May 22, 1945. As a prisoner of the Germans he had been taken to the mass graves at Katyn, together with some other prisoners-of-war. He made the following observations which he revealed to nobody before his release:

1. The bodies wore winter uniforms.
2. The victims' boots and clothing were of excellent quality and showed no signs of wear.
3. "This was the way I saw it," continued van Vliet in his own words. "If the Germans had been responsible for the murders, they would have taken place at the time when the Germans invaded the Smolensk area, in other words in July and August 1941, and then the clothes and shoes would have looked much more used because they would have been worn for two years more. I had had personal experience in that connection. I wore out two pairs of shoes in two years while I was a prisoner (and they were army issue!), and those two years represent more or less the difference in time between the German and the Russian claims for the date of the massacre. So I was convinced without any doubt of Soviet guilt."

General Bissel, head of the United States Information Services, stifled the

- 7 -

aufgefundenen Briefschaften, Tagebüchern, Zeitungen usw. ergibt sich, daß die Erschießungen in den Monaten März und April 1940 stattgefunden haben. Hiermit stehen in völliger Übereinstimmung die im Protokoll geschilderten Befunde an den Massengräbern und den einzelnen Leichen der polnischen Offiziere.

(Dr. Speleers) (Dr. Markov) (Dr. Tramsen)

(Dr. Saxén) (Dr. Palmieri) (Dr. Miloslavich)

(Dr. de Burlet) (Dr. Hajek) (Dr. Birkle)

(Dr. Naville) (Dr. Šubik) (Dr. Orsós)

△ The final page of the report of the European committee, bearing the signatures of its 12 delegates.

◁◁△ Careful scrutiny of documents and personal effects found on the bodies.

◁◁▽ The bodies of Generals Smorawinski and Bochaterewicz are prepared for proper burial with the honours due to their rank.

▽ Checking the nationality. All were found to be Poles.

△ and ▷ Polish and French posters capitalising on the Katyn atrocity. The grim facts lent themselves readily to anti-Soviet propaganda.

report by Colonel van Vliet and went as far as ordering him to make absolutely no mention to anybody of his observations on the slaughter-house of Katyn. But did the former act on his own initiative, basing his decisions on reasons of major state interest about which he was not competent to judge? It seems reasonable to doubt this and to doubt it very strongly, because such a procedure is at variance with the normal practice of secret services.

Russia avoids the issue

Furthermore, and to bring this macabre question to a close, the extreme wariness shown by Soviet historical writing recently is noteworthy. When dealing with the breaking-off of diplomatic relations between Moscow and the Polish Government-in-Exile, the *Great Patriotic War* tells us simply that the U.S.S.R. could no longer tolerate the campaign of calumny indulged in at her expense by General Sikorski and his colleagues. But the history is very careful not to inform its readers of what these calumnies consisted and the name of Katyn is not even mentioned.

Not only was the question of the massacre removed from the attention of the Nuremberg court, but in Moscow, historians still attempt to remove it from the judgement of history!

CHAPTER 104

Cairo prelude

At the Quebec Conference, as we have noted, it was decided to entrust an American general with the command of Operation "Overlord". President Roosevelt's first idea was to appoint General Marshall to this post and make Eisenhower Marshall's successor as the U.S. Army Chief-of-Staff. Clearly he had no Machiavellian intentions, as can be seen from his letter of September 20, 1943 to the veteran General Pershing, who had protested against this appointment:

"I think it is only a fair thing to give George a chance in the field–and because of the nature of the job we shall still have the benefit of his strategical ability. The best way I can express it is to tell you that I want George to be the Pershing of the Second World War–and he cannot be that if we keep him here."

Pershing, who had commanded the American Expeditionary Force in World War I, had expressed his opposition because he considered this appointment would certainly disorganise the Pentagon, and the President's solution would only give Eisenhower the vaguely defined powers of a stop-gap commander. Moreover, Admiral King stated (in spite of the fact that this solution would have strengthened his position), "We have a winning combination here in Washington. Why break it up?" This was plain common sense, and General H. H. Arnold, the commander of the U.S. Army Air Forces, shared his views. Marshall himself remained completely unperturbed during this debate, and only concerned himself with the Allies' victory. Referring to a dispatch which he composed on this matter with General Marshall, Admiral Leahy wrote as follows:

"Never once while we were working on this cable, in our personal conversations, or in the many discussions in the Joint Chiefs of Staff about supreme command did he utter one word that would indicate his own desires."

As soon as the President's intentions were known, they caused some flurry in the American press, amongst whose members Roosevelt had enemies as well as friends. Some of them even thought that under the influence of Harry Hopkins, Felix Frankfurter, Samuel Rosenmann, and David K. Niles, he had decided to exclude Marshall from the conduct of the war, under cover of a flattering appointment, and to take it over himself. The assumption was both mischievous and absurd: Roosevelt's only purpose was to give Marshall the supreme command which would distinguish him permanently in the view of posterity.

These plans, however, gave the persons concerned a suitable opportunity for

∇ *Cheers for Churchill on his arrival at Alexandria on the* Renown. *On the journey he had called at Algiers where he invested Generals Eisenhower and Alexander with a special version of the North Africa ribbon bearing the numbers 1 and 8, signifying the two British armies in the campaign.*

▲▲ *Generalissimo Chiang Kai-shek with Sir George Cunningham, the Governor of the North Western Frontier Province, visiting Jamrud Fort in the Khyber Pass.*
▲ *Lord Louis Mountbatten joined Chiang Kai-shek and his wife when they visited a training centre in eastern India.*
▷ *With their son Major Chiang Wei-Kuo, the Generalissimo and Mme. Chiang watch an artillery demonstration given by American trained and equipped Chinese troops.*

making a few typically American jokes:

"A light note in the midst of the unpleasant ruckus was struck by a monitoring of a Nazi propaganda broadcast from Paris which said: 'General George C. Marshall, the U.S. Chief of Staff, has been dismissed. President Roosevelt has taken over his command. This occurred two days ago, but has not yet been commented on in Washington.'

"Marshall passed this on to Hopkins with the note: 'Dear Harry: Are you responsible for pulling this fast one on me? G.C.M.'

"Hopkins showed this to Roosevelt, who then wrote in pencil on the same note: 'Dear George–Only true in part–I am now Chief of Staff, but *you* are President. F.D.R.' "

However, the British Government did not approve of the American solution. Roosevelt's latest idea had been to put the preparations and conduct not only of "Overlord" but also of the Mediterranean theatre in Marshall's hands. The British, however, were well aware of Marshall's negative attitude to the prosecution of the offensive in Italy, not to mention the liberation of Rhodes and the Dodecanese, and so they would not accept such an extension of Marshall's powers. They rightly thought that the task was too heavy for one man to undertake, although they admitted that Marshall had an enormous capacity for work in addition to his other obvious abilities.

Russian suspicions

In the Allies' delay in appointing an "Overlord" commander, Stalin sensed a treacherous manoeuvre by the two governments to free themselves from their obligation to open a Second Front in Western Europe, and at the Teheran Conference he did not conceal his suspicions from Churchill and Roosevelt. Soviet historians took up the same theme after Stalin's death, and even after "destalinization", with an enthusiasm worthy of a better cause. In fact all the documents show that Washington claimed the command of the Second Front for an American to ensure that it would be launched on the agreed date, and that Marshall was Roosevelt's choice because he would see that this was done.

In spite of Roosevelt's and Hopkins's championing of "Overlord", they made a false move in choosing their candidate, but it would be adding ignorance to calumny to suggest that this move was deliberately deceitful.

Towards a summit conference

A meeting of the American President and the heads of the Soviet and United Kingdom Governments was now due to plan the execution of the decisions reached at Quebec and to co-ordinate the views of the three great powers regarding the joint future conduct of the war and the post-war settlement of Europe. The Soviet offensive, which was at its height, prevented Stalin from going further than Teheran. Roosevelt did not want to risk the constitutional period of ten days, during which an American president can veto Congress legislation, passing during his absence, and suggested Cairo, Asmara (the capital of the former Italian colony of Eritrea), or Basra on the Persian Gulf as the venue.

But Stalin was obdurate and Roosevelt acceded to his wishes. It was said that Stalin had wanted to test Roosevelt's strength of will. This is quite possible, but it should also be mentioned that Stalin kept a tight rein on his chief subordinates; in checking their operations he went into greater detail than would be the case in Western armies; moreover, Soviet commanders took no initiative without consulting him on the telephone and this would not have been possible if Stalin had travelled further than Teheran.

During his visit to Moscow, when making preparations for the conference there, Anthony Eden became aware of Stalin's military rôle:

"Stalin did not want to leave Russia and Molotov told me that his presence was indispensable to the conduct of the fighting on the Russian front. I was rather sceptical about this, but it was probably true. For instance, on the evening when we were discussing convoys, Stalin was called to the telephone in the room where we were talking, a very rare occurrence. Our excellent interpreter, Major Birse, told me afterwards that from Stalin's end of the conversation he was giving a decision about targets to bombard in the Crimea."

Roosevelt, Harry Hopkins, Admirals Leahy and King, Generals Marshall and Arnold, and their principal assistants embarked on the new fast battleship *Iowa*, which set sail from Hampton Roads during the night of November 12–13. According to Leahy:

"President Roosevelt had no superstitions about the figure '13', which many people regard as an ill omen, but he did share the sailors' superstition that Friday is an unlucky day on which to start a long voyage. So the huge USS *Iowa* remained at her berth Friday night, November 12, 1943, and did not get under way for Oran, the first leg of the trip to Cairo and Teheran, until 12.01 am, Saturday, November 13."

The *Iowa* landed them on November 20 at Mers el Kébir, where General Dwight D. Eisenhower was waiting for them, "smiling broadly" as Leahy noted. In 24 hours in Carthage they were able to get a full briefing on the operational prospects in Italy. They landed at Cairo in a four-engined transport plane at 0930 hours on November 22. Churchill and his general staff, including Admiral of the Fleet Sir Andrew Cunningham, who had succeeded Sir Dudley Pound (he had died on October 21), had already been in Cairo for 48 hours. Generalissimo Chiang Kai-shek, with his influential wife and his chief of general staff, General Joseph Stilwell, who was also Lord Mountbatten's deputy, and three Chinese generals had also just arrived.

▽ *"Madame was a study in herself; a queer character in which sex and politics seemed to predominate, both being used to achieve her ends." So Brooke described Mme. Chiang when he met her at Cairo. She acted as her husband's interpreter, and Brooke added after the war: "She was the only woman amongst a very large gathering of men and was determined to bring into action all the charms nature had blessed her with." Here she is seen apparently achieving her ends with Churchill.*

Training the Chinese army

△ Weapon training under the eyes of an American instructor. Chinese troops practise the variations of bayonet drill.
◁ A U.S. Colonel explains artillery tactics to a group of Chinese officers.
▷ △ The mechanics of a medium machine gun are demonstrated by a U.S. captain.
▷ ▷ △ △ The officers and N.C.O.s of a training establishment in Kwangsi are addressed by Chiang Kai-shek in his capacity as head of state and C.-in-C. of China and her forces.

▷ △ Assisted by an interpreter, a captain briefs a Chinese officer on range practice. Note the China-Burma-India badge on the American's shirt.
▷ Curtiss P-40 Warhawks, sporting their Flying Tiger insignia under guard on their Chinese airstrip.

106

HELP CHINA
China is helping us!
PLEASE GIVE ALL YOU CAN ON
CHINA'S FLAG DAY

The "Sextant" Conference

As soon as its agenda had been decided on, this inter-Allied conference, which was given the title "Sextant", was marked by a sudden clash between Sir Alan Brooke, the obstinate Ulsterman, and the irascible Admiral King. In his diary "Vinegar Joe", as his American Army colleagues nicknamed Stilwell, describes what happened:

"November 23 . . . 2.30 G-mo phoned 'Do not present proposals'. Message that G-mo would come. Then he wouldn't. Then he would. Christ. Brooke got nasty and King got good and sore. King almost climbed over the table at Brooke. God, he was mad. I wish he had socked him."

Doubtless this is exaggerated. A reading of Stilwell's diary shows that he was a scandal-monger and poked fun at every-one in very colourful language, so much so that a few days later President Roose-velt admitted that he had had to ask Stilwell to give up using the nickname "peanut" with which he referred to Chiang Kai-shek.

Priority for Europe

Nevertheless there was a genuine con-flict, as Sir Arthur Bryant writes in his valuable commentary to Lord Alan-brooke's war diaries:

"For, with the C.I.G.S. as spokesman, the British Chiefs of Staff had strongly opposed the American proposal to discuss the South-East Asia campaign before agreeing on the plans for assailing the Axis fortress in Europe and the overall strategy for the war against Japan. Only when these had been settled, the C.I.G.S. had maintained, would it be practicable to allocate assault shipping for the very minor operation against the Andaman Isles–*Buccaneer*.

"The Americans had listened with impatience to Brooke's formidable battery of statistical evidence to prove that no assault-craft could be spared for even the smallest operation in the Indian Ocean until after Eisenhower's and Alexander's impending sea attack on the German flank in Italy and then only if *'Overlord'* were postponed from May till July to give time for the shipping sent from the Mediterranean to the Bay of Bengal to be brought back to Europe."

Therefore the British Chiefs-of-Staff, who had already put Churchill off the Sumatra operation, expressed their opposition to Operation "Buccaneer" (in spite of Lord Mountbatten's arguments) and preferred the Allied operations in Western Europe. Their opposition became all the stronger as the result of the deplorable impression made by the Chinese delegation when they got down to brass tacks and discussed China's share in the "triphibious" offensive they proposed to launch against Japan in the South-East Asian Theatre.

Chiang Kai-shek's evasions

"The British obviously did not have the same deep interest in China that we had," Admiral Leahy wrote. This was quite correct, but he also noted that Chiang Kai-shek showed neither agreement nor disagreement during the session when Lord Mountbatten explained his opera-tional plan for reconquering Burma. Matters became even worse during the session of November 24; when they were asked to state how and with what forces their armies would join in the planned offensive, the Chinese Generalissimo's chiefs-of-staff simply went on repeating: "We wish to know your intentions!"

Deferential as they were, these repeated excuses exasperated Brooke; he was not impressed by Chiang Kai-shek's per-sonality which he described (he was also a keen naturalist) as follows:

"The Generalissimo reminded me of a cross between a pine-martin and a ferret. A shrewd, foxy sort of face. Evidently with no grasp of war in its larger aspects, but determined to get the best of all bargains."

As for Madame Chiang Kai-shek, who was present at the conference discussions and meddled in what did not concern her, her charm left the British officers cold.

"Buccaneer" or not?

In the Anglo-American dispute, Admiral King's position can be explained easily. Operation "Buccaneer" would have a certain blood-letting effect on the Japanese naval and air forces just at the time when the U.S. 5th Fleet would be

◁ A fund-raising poster for China. She had suffered longer than any other ally in her war with Japan, and in 1942 she seemed to be the only one to have scored any successes.

▽ Admiral of the Fleet Sir Andrew Cunningham. On the death of Admiral Pound in late 1943, Cunningham became First Sea Lord.

▽▽ Mountbatten with General Joseph W. Stilwell. Stilwell had been in charge of the training of Chinese units and their operations in northern Burma, but Mountbatten was made Supreme Allied Commander, South-East Asia.

pressing home its attack on the Caroline Islands and the Marianas in the Central Pacific Area. Marshall supported this view and would not accept Brooke's argument, attempting as it did to show that the Andaman Islands operation would prejudice Normandy. For the last 18 months Marshall had been a convinced supporter of the Second Front, and it was still on the cards that he might command it.

To resolve this apparent contradiction, his argument can be surmised as follows: the landing-craft for the Bay of Bengal, in particular 69 tank landing-craft, would be withdrawn from the Mediterranean. Their removal would not prejudice the success of Operation "Overlord"; although it might prevent the British from making progress in the Italian campaign, Marshall certainly did not regard this as a disadvantage, as he did not think there could be any connection between the Italian operations and the future offensive to be launched on the following May 1 in the Seine Bay.

Leahy, on the other hand, was worried about the strategic consequences of a Chinese collapse brought about by the Japanese.

Roosevelt favours "decolonisation"

President Roosevelt was now looking towards the future, long after the end of the war. Chiang Kai-shek's China, together with the U.S.A., the U.S.S.R., and the U.K., was to be one of the four pillars supporting a world structure which would protect all the peoples of the world and would give them the benefits of liberty, democracy, justice, and peace. In the Far East, this programme necessitated:

1. French withdrawal from Indo-China. Roosevelt was already planning to give China a share in great responsibilities. He revealed his thoughts to General Stilwell, who noted on November 25, 1943;

"His (F.D.R.'s) plan for French Indo-China – three commissioners – Chinese, British, American. Not to go back to France."

2. Hong Kong becoming a free port. On December 6, reminding Stilwell that his grandfather had spent 15 years of his life in China, Roosevelt told him, referring to the Chinese:

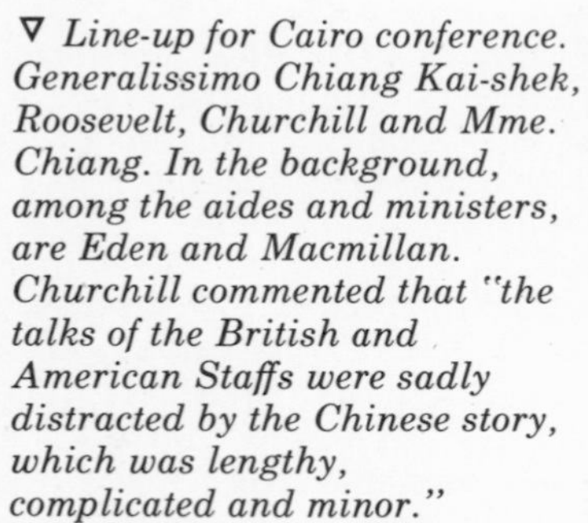

▽ *Line-up for Cairo conference. Generalissimo Chiang Kai-shek, Roosevelt, Churchill and Mme. Chiang. In the background, among the aides and ministers, are Eden and Macmillan. Churchill commented that "the talks of the British and American Staffs were sadly distracted by the Chinese story, which was lengthy, complicated and minor."*

"They really like us and just between ourselves, they *don't* like the British. Now we haven't the same aims as the British out there. For instance, Hong Kong. Now, I have a plan to make Hong Kong a free port: free to the commerce of all nations–of the world! But let's raise the Chinese flag there first, and then Chiang can the next day make a grand gesture and make it a free port. That's the way to handle that!"

3. Indonesia a trusteeship independent of the Dutch. It seems unlikely that Stilwell exaggerated when he reported these remarks. On June 1, 1942 when President Roosevelt received Molotov at the White House, he told him on his own account, without prompting from his guest, that the Dutch would not return to Batavia and that Indonesia would be put under the trusteeship of the U.S.A., the U.S.S.R., Great Britain and China until she attained political maturity. And in Churchill's absence he intended making a similar remark to Stalin about India. This is how Franklin Roosevelt light-heartedly set American policy on a "decolonisation" course at the end of which, for the thousands of millions of dollars spent, over 1,000 million people, far from being freed from fear and hunger, were to be subjected to tyranny and megalomania, to maladministration and to abuse of trust, all without being consulted.

△ *Russo-American co-operation. U.S. bomber pilots operating from a Russian airfield pose with bombs suitably chalked up for the camera.*

Several such decisions were made at the Cairo Conference. According to the published diaries of those present Churchill, when he put the liberation of the Aegean, the assault on Rhodes, and the intervention of Turkey on the agenda, did not support the point of view of his chiefs-of-staff very effectively. In fact Marshall, King, and Arnold, who received Roosevelt's and Hopkins's full support, won all along the line. Moreover when General and Madame Chiang Kai-shek left for Chungking, they were sure they could rely on a vigorous Anglo-American attack in South-East Asia, including a landing in the Andaman Islands.

Undoubtedly the Americans must have been all the more pleased with the results of the conference, since in spite of Brooke's obstinacy they had managed to avoid any positive commitment to include Chinese participation in this vast cycle of operations. But at Teheran Stalin, for easily understandable reasons, supported the reservations with which the British chiefs-of-staff had hedged their agreement.

STALIN
RUSSIA'S OVERLORD

From Georgian political agitator to party boss.
1. Joseph Vissarionovich Stalin, successor to Lenin and one of the eight men who spurred on the October Revolution.
2. From the Tsarist police files: Stalin's record as a subversive agitator, complete with finger-prints, photographs, and full details of past convictions. He was exiled to Siberia twice.
3. Stalin with Lenin and Kalinin. When Lenin fell ill in 1922, Stalin became one of the five committee members who assumed collective leadership in his stead.

To Roosevelt he was "Joe", a man with whom one could "do business"; to Churchill he was first a much-needed ally, and then a long-term menace even greater than Hitler. And Joseph Stalin wasted no time in exploiting the differences between his allies to the full. This came naturally, after decades of consolidation and advancement which had made him Lenin's unchallenged successor and absolute master of the Soviet Union.

Stalin started life as Joseph Vissarionovich Dzhugashvili, the son of a Georgian shoemaker. Born at Gori on December 21, 1879, he was originally intended to study for the priesthood in the Georgian Orthodox Church. In 1894 he entered the theological seminary at Tiflis and soon made his mark as an industrious and keen-minded student. However, he soon began to dabble in socialist ideas and was expelled from the seminary for "disloyal" views, in 1899.

Dzhugashvili threw himself into the revolutionary movement and became an enthusiastic supporter of Lenin's journal *Iskra* ("The Spark"). Elected to the Social Democratic Party in 1901

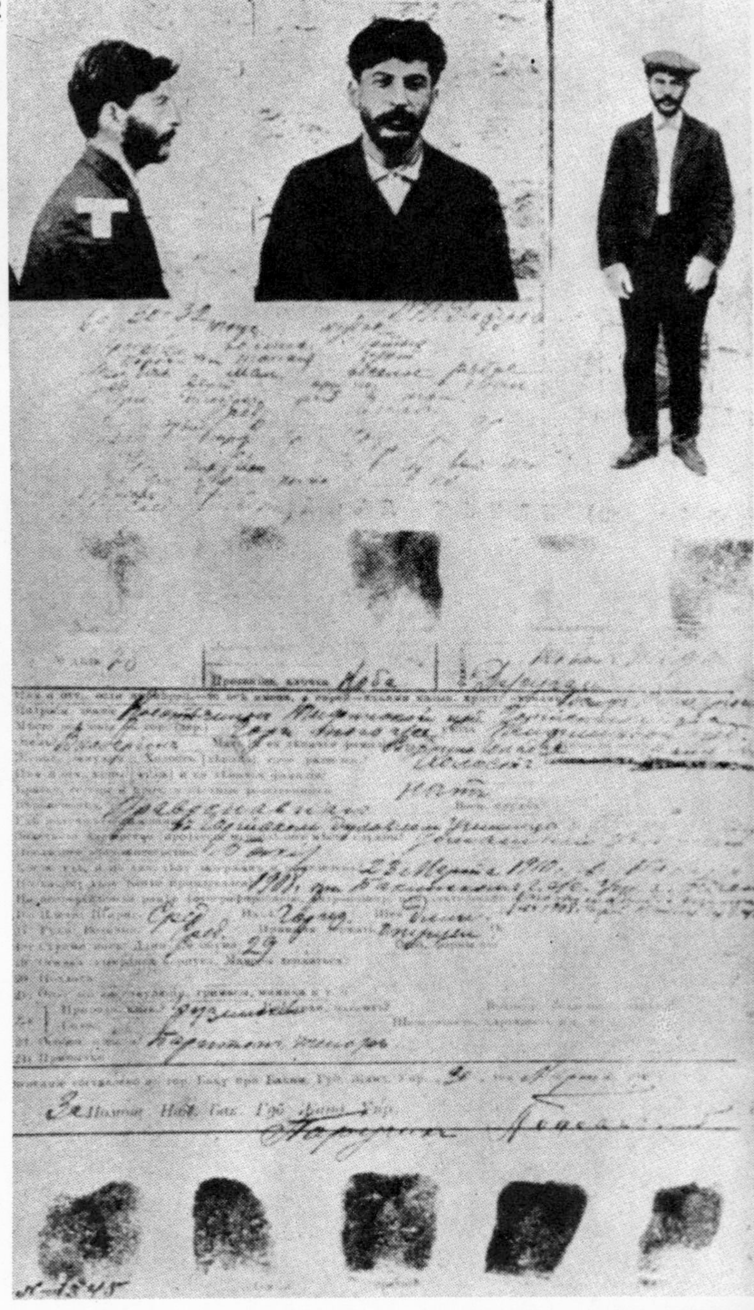

4. Biding his time. Stalin with Lenin in Gorky in 1922. With Zinoviev, Kamenev, Bukharin, and Rykov, Stalin embarked on a cautious policy in economics and foreign affairs. Lenin remained as an elder statesman until his death in January 1924.
5. Ten years after Lenin's death, and Stalin has moved into a position of prominence. In the front row Ordzhonikidze, Stalin, Molotov, and Kirov whose assassination was used as one of the justifications for the purges of 1934-1938. Back row: Yenukidze (later purged), Voroshilov, Kaganovich, and Kuibishev, who died in an alleged medical murder. His ruthlessness with his comrades was reflected in the rigorous way he enforced a policy of industrialisation and collectivisation which displaced about 25,000,000 peasants. He justified these moves by stating that Russia was 50 or 100 years behind other countries, and they undoubtedly gave the U.S.S.R. the industrial resources necessary to prosecute the war.

8

he was soon arrested as a subversive and was deported to Siberia; but he escaped and returned to Tiflis shortly after the Social Democrats had split into the Bolshevik and Menshevik factions. Dzhugashvili supported the Bolsheviks and first met Lenin in 1905. Between then and 1914 he emerged as the Bolshevik leader of Baku and participated in party congresses held in Sweden and Britain.

In 1912 Lenin and the Bolsheviks finally broke with the Mensheviks and formed a central party, with Lenin making

6. *"Uncle Joe" as seen in a contemporary propaganda poster.*
7. *Stalin with Maxim Gorky the writer. Stalin was active in the preparations for the October Revolution as the editor of the party paper* Pravda.
8. *Molotov and Stalin and other party leaders on Lenin's tomb. Stalin was less concerned with revolutionary ideals than with maintaining his own authority over the Communist world.*
9. *Dictator at work: Stalin signs a death warrant. Opposition was removed by trial or murder.*

Dzhugashvili a member of the central committee. He was the first editor of the party newspaper *Pravda,* which appeared in 1912. In the following year he was arrested again and spent the next four years in Siberia, where he adopted the pseudonym "Stalin", the "man of steel".

Returning from Siberia in March 1917, Stalin resumed the editorship of *Pravda*. He played no direct part in the Bolshevik revolution of 1917, but Lenin appointed him Commissar of Nationalities after the Bolshevik seizure of power. Later he was appointed Commissar of the Workers' and Peasants' Inspectorate, with the power to supervise the other branches of the new administration. In the civil war (1918-1920) Stalin was a member of the Council of Defence, a political commissar, and inspector of fronts. He played a key rôle in the defence of the young Bolshevik state, organising the defence of Petrograd (later Leningrad), Tsaritsyn (later Stalingrad), and Orel. He also served during the war with Poland in 1920. It was during these years that his clash with Trotsky, the founder of the Red Army and Lenin's generally-accepted heir-apparent, began. In 1922 Stalin was appointed secretary-general of the party–an important stage in his advancement, for it gave him eventual control over both party and government.

After Lenin's death (January 1924) the power struggle began in earnest, with Stalin, Zinoviev, and Kamenev closing ranks against Trotsky. While extending his control over the party by abolishing its freedom of expression, Stalin managed to oust Trotsky. He then turned against Zinoviev and Kamenev by allying himself with the three key party "right-wingers", Bukharin, Rykov, and Tomsky. After expelling Trotsky, Zinoviev, and Kamenev from the party he turned against his former allies and meted out similar treatment to them. When he expelled Trotsky from Russia in 1929 Stalin remained as the undisputed overlord of the U.S.S.R.

In the next decade Stalin's energy and utter ruthlessness transformed Russia from its backward state into a modern industrial power. It was an agonising process, involving the forcible transfer of millions of peasants to industrial centres, but without it Russia would never have been able to survive the war. At the same time, however, the despotic nature of his rule revealed itself in the mass purges of 1936-38, which broke the last shards of possible opposition.

The crisis of 1941 brought out all Stalin's bedrock qualities: tenacity, iron nerves, and willpower. These qualities he never lost–and they paid dividends.

10. *The last parade. The generals at the foot of Lenin's tomb in this May Day Parade were nearly all to be executed as traitors. The only survivors, Budenny and Voroshilov, were unable to cope with the German advances of 1941, though Voroshilov later became a capable diplomat. The generals are, from left to right, Tukhachevsky, Byelov, Voroshilov, Yegorov, and Budenny. In his purges Stalin destroyed the "brains" of the Red Army of the 1930's.*
11. *Leaders and advisors. Stalin and Churchill with Hopkins and Eden at Teheran.*
12. *Stalin's son Vasily as a pilot during the war. He was to die in disgrace in a home for alcoholics.*

CHAPTER 105

The Teheran conference

▷ *A new angle on the Teheran story. Cameramen cluster to get their pictures at a press reception. Churchill complained afterwards that the arrangements for his arrival provided "no kind of defence against two or three determined men with pistols or a bomb."*

On November 27 the American President, the British Premier, and their aides left at dawn for Teheran, where the "Eureka" Conference was due to be held. When they flew over the Suez Canal, Brooke and Cunningham spotted the five battleships of the Italian fleet put out of commission according to the armistice agreement, and at anchor in the Bitter Lakes. On arrival in the Persian capital, the American delegation, for security reasons, moved to an annexe of the Soviet Embassy, as Stalin had informed Roosevelt that the U.S. legation, into which it had first moved, was at the other end of the town and that over such a long distance an assassination attempt on the President was to be feared. Molotov, he said, was already on the track of some conspiracy.

The security of the President and his aides was therefore guaranteed, but those involved were not allowed to forget it for a moment. Hopkins stated:

"The servants who made their beds and cleaned their rooms were all members of the highly efficient NKVD, the secret police, and expressive bulges were plainly discernible in the hip pockets under their white coats. It was a nervous time for Michael F. Reilly and his own White House secret service men, who were trained to suspect *everybody* and who did not like to admit into the President's presence anyone who was armed with as much as a gold toothpick."

The conduct of the war and the European settlement were the main agenda for the Teheran Conference; in addition Cordell Hull, the American Secretary of State, Eden, the head of the Foreign Office, and Molotov, the Soviet Foreign Minister, who had just met in Moscow, took part in the conversations between Roosevelt, Churchill, and Stalin when they started to discuss post-war questions in general and Poland and Germany in particular.

Stalin: strategic genius?

The first session of the "Eureka" Conference opened in a drawing room in the Soviet Embassy at 1630 hours on November 28. A little earlier, Stalin had met Roosevelt privately; Roosevelt had explained his views on the reorganisation of the world, particularly the future of India, and begged him not to mention this problem in Churchill's presence.

Flanked by Molotov and Marshal Voroshilov, Stalin was resplendent in a uniform, according to Lord Moran "that looks as if it has not been worn before, and gives the impression that it has been specially designed for the occasion. It looks, too, as if the tailor has put a shelf on each shoulder, and on it has dumped a lot of gold lace with white stars. And there is a broad red stripe down the trousers, which are immaculately creased. All this is crowned with a dreadful hat, smothered with gold braid."

Churchill's doctor concluded this satirical portrait by admitting he was curious to know how Stalin's mind worked. Brooke had this opportunity in Teheran, Moscow (October 1944), Yalta, and Potsdam. Writing in 1946, he replied as follows to this question:

"I had already formed a very high idea of his ability, force of character and shrewdness, but did not know yet whether he was also a strategist . . .

"During this meeting and all the subsequent ones we had with Stalin, I rapidly grew to appreciate the fact that he had a military brain of the highest calibre. Never once in any of his statements did he make any strategic error, nor did he ever fail to appreciate all the implications of a situation with a quick and unerring eye. In this respect he stood out compared with his two colleagues. Roosevelt never made any great pretence at being a strategist and left either Marshall or Leahy to talk for him. Winston, on the other hand, was more erratic, brilliant at times, but too impulsive and inclined to favour unsuitable plans without giving them the preliminary deep thought they required."

Before he even left for Teheran, Harry Hopkins, President Roosevelt's right-hand man, was dissatisfied with the result of the "Sextant" Conference and was "quite fierce" when he said to Lord Moran, who took down his remark:

"Sure, we are preparing for a battle at

△▷ The presentation of the "Stalingrad Sword" to Stalin. It had been forged to commemorate the defence of Stalingrad, and its display in London had drawn large crowds. Writing of the presentation Churchill said, "When, after a few sentences of explanation, I handed the splendid weapon to Marshal Stalin he raised it in a most impressive gesture to his lips and kissed the scabbard. He then passed it to Voroshilov, who dropped it. It was carried from the room with great solemnity by a Russian guard of honour. As this procession moved away I saw the President sitting at the side of the room, obviously stirred by the ceremony."
▷ Stalin chuckles as Churchill takes out a cigar. Though the photographs seem to show the Allies in agreement, Brooke, commenting on Stalin's intransigence and the strain of working with interpreters, said "After listening to the arguments put forward during the last two days I felt like entering a lunatic asylum or a nursing-home!"

Teheran. You will find us lining up with the Russians."

In fact, the Americans and the Russians concerted to stop Churchill and the British chiefs-of-staff, who recommended continuing operations in Italy until the Leghorn–Rimini line was reached.

Stalin's greed

In this discussion one may have to admit, as Soviet historians still maintain and as Hopkins and Marshall seemed to think at the time, that the Prime Minister and the C.I.G.S. were trying with this specious manoeuvre to defuse Operation "Overlord" without openly repudiating its principle.

According to Stalin, the Mediterranean strategy favoured by the British would lead to the waste of Allied troops, even supposing that Turkey would agree to give up her neutrality, which he did not believe. The centre of Germany was not to be reached through the Balkans, nor in fact through Italy, since, when the Apennines had been crossed, the Allies would stand in front of the virtually impassable barrier of the Alps, where the famous Suvorov was defeated in 1799.

"He said he thought OVERLORD should be considered the basis for all operations in 1944 and that after the capture of Rome the forces used there should be sent into Southern France to provide a diversionary operation in support of OVERLORD. He even felt that it might be better to abandon the capture of Rome altogether, leaving ten divisions to hold the present line in Italy, and using the rest of the Allied force for the invasion of Southern France. He said it had been the experience of the Red Army that it was better to launch an offensive from two converging directions, forcing the enemy to move his reserves from one front to the other. Therefore, he favoured simultaneous operations in Northern and Southern France, rather than the 'scattering' of forces in the Eastern Mediterranean."

And the next day, when Churchill failed to agree to all the assumptions of his arguments, Stalin abruptly cried out, as Admiral Leahy reported:

"Do you really believe in 'Overlord', or are you stalling on it to make us feel better?"

The full record of the session, as condensed by Robert E. Sherwood in his *The White House Papers of Harry L. Hopkins* and Churchill in his memoirs, somewhat tones down the Soviet dictator's question, but, for obvious reasons, we shall keep to the American admiral's version.

In any event, the British representatives' arguments in the discussion were not improvised for the occasion; on the contrary, they corresponded to strategic conceptions whose value cannot be underestimated. When Stalin said he saw no

need for the Western Allies to capture Rome, Churchill replied:

"General Alexander, who under General Eisenhower, was commanding the Fifteenth Army Group in Italy, aimed not only at taking Rome, but at destroying or capturing ten or eleven German divisions."

Six months were still to pass before "Overlord" was launched, and there was no question of letting the enemy have freedom of action in the meantime. This would be a serious error, as Brooke wrote in his diary on the evening of November 29:

"Voroshilov's main theme was that the cross-Channel operation must have preference over all others, and that the date must remain May 1st. In vain I argued that by closing operations in the Mediterranean German forces would be free to proceed to other theatres."

On the other hand, contrary to what Stalin had maintained, Churchill had as yet no intention of extending the offensive from the Apennines (between Leghorn and Rimini) as far as the Alps. When the Leghorn–Rimini line was reached, the victory would be exploited either by a landing in the south of France or by crossing the Adriatic, as suggested by President Roosevelt, to give assistance to Marshal Tito.

The debate, which was to become more and more bitter, was settled behind Roosevelt's back at a private meeting between Churchill and Stalin on November 30, the former's 69th birthday.

In short, Churchill told Stalin, they were faced with a dilemma: either to keep to the date fixed for launching "Overlord" or to continue the Mediterranean offensive. But, as often happens, this was a false dilemma, because the reason they were forced to choose between these irritating alternatives was, as Brooke noted more frankly than Churchill could say, that the Americans had put the cart before the horse when they promised Chiang Kai-shek Operation "Buccaneer" before obtaining the agreement of the U.S.S.R. Consequently, Brooke added:

"It was not a choice between the Mediterranean and the date of 'Overlord' but between the Bay of Bengal and the date of 'Overlord'."

It was possible therefore to reconcile the British and Soviet positions by keeping in the Mediterranean the landing craft which the Americans wished to send through the Suez Canal to the Far East. Stalin, who expected nothing useful to come from Chiang Kai-shek, had no difficulty in supporting this argument.

Russian aid against Japan?

The Americans did not appear to be unduly shocked by Stalin's change of attitude. In fact they had obtained a formal promise of support against Japan from him, which was to be fulfilled as

◁ *"The Big Tree" as the world saw them. With Molotov and Eden in the background they were directing the war, and seeking the peace. But according to Brooke it was a case of "the more politicians you put together to settle the prosecution of the war, the longer you postpone its conclusion."*

soon as the Third Reich, defeated by the concerted offensive of the three Allied powers, had been driven to unconditional surrender.

There was a final military question to settle. At the session of November 29 Stalin asked point-blank: "Who is going to command 'Overlord'?", adding harshly that he would not believe in the reality of the Second Front until a commander had been chosen to lead it. Roosevelt now made an equivocal reply. In fact at this time he had not given up the idea of appointing Marshall nor succeeded in convincing those who, like Admiral King, thought that a change at the top would bring grave disadvantages.

The military decisions

Finally, the following compromise was arrived at:

1. Operation "Buccaneer" would be abandoned;
2. the Italian front would be kept under pressure to prevent the Germans from withdrawing reinforcements for the Russian front; the Leghorn–Rimini line remained the offensive's final objective;
3. the date for "Overlord" was postponed to June 1 so that the Channel crossing and the assault on the Bay of the Seine would coincide with the Soviet summer offensive; and
4. the Second Front would open at the same time as the Allies landed in the south of France. The required amphibious transport would be collected for the simultaneous landing of two of the six divisions taking part in the "Anvil" operation.

The post-war world

As regards the redrawing of the map of Europe and the setting up of a new international order, the discussions between Stalin, Churchill, and Roosevelt, assisted by Molotov, Anthony Eden, and Cordell Hull, never again reached such a degree of unanimity for the simple reason that the British Prime Minister and the U.S. President almost consistently gave in to the slightest whim of their Soviet ally.

By an agreement at the end of July 1941 between the Kremlin and the Polish Government in Exile, the U.S.S.R. had declared that it renounced the territorial advantages conferred on it by the German-Soviet treaties of August 23 and September 28, 1939. For General Sikorski, this clause indicated that after the German defeat, the Russo-Polish frontier of the Treaty of Riga (March 12,1921) would be restored; it had to some extent been confirmed by the non-aggression pact freely concluded between the Moscow and Warsaw governments on July 25, 1932.

For Stalin and Molotov this agreement meant in November 1943 that the frontiers of the two states would be redrawn, on the

Two views of the Allies.
◁ A Soviet poster illustrating a quote by Stalin: "The Red Army with the armies of our Allies will break the back of the Fascist beast."
△ A German poster displayed in Poland: "The German soldier is the guarantor of victories." Here Russia becomes a ravening wolf, the American eagle a balding vulture, and Britain (perfidious Albion) a snake.

▷ A leaflet published by the United States Information Office gives a condensed version of the Teheran talks. Few countries realised that their frontiers had been realigned and their post-war fates decided.

basis of the Curzon Line, so called because it had been traced on the map in July 1920 by Lord Curzon, then head of the Foreign Office. The Poles, however, had never recognised it. The "Bolsheviks", as they were called at the time, hoped to conquer the whole of Poland, and had advanced beyond the line that Britain and France had offered them as the price of stopping hostilities. They had good cause to regret it, as on the following August 6 (1920) the Red Army reached Warsaw and was then routed by Marshal Piłsudski.

Certainly the frontier of March 12, 1921 had brought under Polish domination territories and populations which the Russians had claimed as theirs for centuries, but the Curzon Line would have settled these disputed areas to the sole advantage of Russia, without regard for the overlapping populations. On the other hand, whilst Stalin and Molotov claimed the Ukrainian and Belorussian provinces of the Polish Republic for the U.S.S.R., they gave their populations no right of option. But whilst the U.S.S.R.'s right to the Curzon Line frontier may appear doubtful, Churchill's and Roosevelt's right to decide Poland's future high-handedly without consulting her leaders, and to commit Great Britain and the U.S.A. respectively on their own initiative, was completely non-existent. And the Prime Minister, when he suggested that Stalin should try to draw the future Polish-Soviet frontier, admitted this:

"I have no power from Parliament, nor, I believe, has the President, to define any frontier lines. But we might now, in Teheran, see if the three heads of Government, working in agreement, could form some sort of policy which we could recommend to the Poles and advise them to accept."

They did this very quickly by mutual agreement (subject to certain adjustments to be made later) and the two statesmen promised Stalin they would "advise" Poland to accept the Curzon Line as her eastern frontier. Admittedly she would be compensated in the west for what she gave up in the east. Winston Churchill wrote as follows:

"Personally I thought Poland might move westwards, like soldiers taking two steps 'left close'. If Poland trod on some German toes that could not be helped, but there must be a strong Poland. Poland was an instrument needed in the orchestra of Europe."

Which Europe? Which Poland? one might well ask, reading Churchill's memoirs. It was decided then that after the Allied victory, the Oder would be the frontier between Poland and Germany; Germany would therefore lose Eastern Prussia, Pomerania, the Brandenburg Marches, and part of Silesia. By restricting in this way the gains promised to Warsaw to only a part of Silesia, we have in mind Churchill's question during the discussions concerning the distribution of the Oppeln (Opole) district. As this district was up the river beyond Breslau (Wrocław) this question would have been meaningless, as it had already been decided that the future frontier would leave the Oder at Fürstenberg and would then follow the course of the northern Neisse. As a counterpart to the support they promised to give the Soviet claim to the Curzon Line, Roosevelt and Churchill attempted to obtain Stalin's agreement to resume relations with the Polish Government in London. It appeared to be easier as General Sikorski had been killed in a plane accident on the preceding July 4 and his successor, Stanislas Mikolajczyk, the leader of the Peasant Party, had been less prominently involved in the protest about the Katyn affair. But Stalin was intractable, stating that the Polish Government in Exile had carried on a slanderous campaign against the Soviet Union. The two Allied statesmen did not insist. They were not aware of the paradox of wanting to impose the sacrifice of its eastern frontiers on a Polish Government (with which Moscow refused to maintain normal diplomatic relations) by bringing forward considerations which it knew to be false.

Stalin produced a further argument in support of his posture. He told the others that the future security of the Soviet Union made it imperative that Moscow could count on a "friendly" government in Warsaw. No one retorted that the danger he foresaw of a German return to criminal warfare was imaginary, as they had agreed to occupy the entire Third Reich, divide it, and dismantle its war potential.

Germany to be divided

In Roosevelt's opinion, this aim would be reached if five autonomous states were set up on German soil:

Déclaration

NOUS, LE PRESIDENT DES ETATS-UNIS D'AMERIQUE, LE PREMIER MINISTRE BRITANNIQUE, ET LE CHEF DU GOUVERNEMENT DE L'UNION SOVIETIQUE, VENONS DE CONFERER PENDANT QUATRE JOURS EN CETTE CAPITALE DE NOTRE ALLIE L'IRAN, ET AVONS DEFINI ET CONFIRME NOTRE POLITIQUE COMMUNE.

Nous affirmons notre résolution d'assurer la collaboration de nos peuples dans la guerre comme dans la paix qui suivra.

EN CE QUI CONCERNE LA GUERRE: *les Etats-Majors de nos trois pays ont participé à nos débats communs et nous avons tracé de concert nos plans destinés à assurer la destruction des forces armées allemandes. Nous avons abouti à un complet accord en ce qui concerne l'envergure et la synchronisation des opérations qui seront déclenchées de l'est, de l'ouest et du sud.*

L'accord auquel nous avons abouti ici garantit notre victoire.

EN CE QUI CONCERNE LA PAIX: *nous sommes certains que la concorde qui règne entre nous conduira à une paix durable. Nous sommes entièrement conscients de la responsabilité suprême qui nous incombe, de même qu'à toutes les Nations Unies: celle de bâtir une paix qui sera appuyée de plein gré par la majorité écrasante des peuples de la terre, une paix qui bannira le fléau et l'horreur de la guerre pour de nombreuses générations.*

Nous avons examiné avec nos conseillers diplomatiques les problèmes de l'avenir. Nous ferons appel à la coopération et la participation active de tous les pays, grands et petits, dont les peuples comme nos propres peuples se consacrent de tout leur coeur et de toute leur volonté à la suppression de la tyrannie et de l'esclavage, de l'oppression et de l'intolérance. Nous les accueillerons, à mesure qu'ils choisiront de nous rejoindre, au sein de la famille mondiale des nations démocratiques.

Nulle puissance au monde ne saurait nous empêcher de détruire les armées allemandes sur terre, les sous-marins allemands en mer, les usines de guerre allemandes par la voie des airs.

Notre attaque sera implacable et d'une vigueur sans cesse accrue.

A L'ISSUE DE NOS CORDIAUX ENTRETIENS, NOUS ATTENDONS AVEC CONFIANCE LE JOUR OU TOUS LES PEUPLES DE LA TERRE POURRONT VIVRE LIBREMENT, A L'ABRI DE LA TYRANNIE, SELON LEURS DESIRS RESPECTIFS ET SELON LEUR CONSCIENCE.

Nous sommes venus ici pleins d'espoir et de résolution. Nous repartons unis par l'amitié, la volonté et la communauté de nos buts.

Franklin D Roosevelt
И. Сталин.
Winston S Churchill

SIGNE A TEHERAN LE 1ER DECEMBRE 1943

PUBLIÉ PAR L'OFFICE D'INFORMATION DE GUERRE DES ETATS-UNIS

1. Prussia reduced in size, i.e. to Brandenburg
2. Hannover and Westphalia
3. Hesse and the Rhineland
4. Baden, Bavaria, and Württemberg
5. Saxony, increased at Prussia's expense, whilst as an additional precaution the Ruhr and Saar industrial areas and the Kiel Canal area with Hamburg would be put under United Nations control.

Austria reconstituted

Winston Churchill raised no objection to this plan in principle; he merely suggested, taking up again an idea that had been discussed in 1919, that Bavaria should be separated from the rest of Germany; if it was joined under certain conditions to Austria and Hungary, there would be a consistent and economically viable federal state in the Danube basin. Stalin gave the plan a cold reception, but his audience raised no objections when he claimed Königsberg, with the excuse that it was the only Baltic port that did not freeze over in winter.

Finally Roosevelt, at his own request, was given the opportunity to explain his ideas on the future world organisation which when peace came would replace the old League of Nations. Going from the periphery to the centre there would be:

1. a world consultative assembly where all the member states of the institution would meet periodically;
2. an executive committee including the four Great Powers and representatives of two European states, a Middle East state, a British dominion, a South American republic, and a Far East country. But its competence would be limited to economic, food, health, and other similar matters, and would exclude security questions; and
3. finally, only the four Great Powers would be admitted within the inner circle; Roosevelt called them the "four policemen". Thus it would be the duty of the U.S.A., Great Britain, the U.S.S.R., and China to impose peace on the world. If an aggression were threatened, the four policemen would punish the offending state with a graduated scale of sanctions going as far as aerial bombardment and the invasion of its territory.

▽ Churchill's 69th birthday, which on November 30 came as finale to the Teheran conference. For Churchill it was "a memorable occasion in my life. On my right sat the President of the United States on my left the master of Russia. Together we controlled a large preponderance of the naval and three-quarters of all the air forces in the world, and could direct armies of nearly twenty millions of men."

Support from Stalin

If one considers the questions Stalin put when he heard this programme, one must admit that, determined as he was not to sacrifice the smallest part of Soviet national sovereignty on the altar of the new world organisation, he immediately understood the immense possibilities of infiltration, intervention, subversion, and conquest naïvely contrived for him by the American plan.

The "four policemen" system opened the doors wide for him: on the one hand, the continental European powers would not be admitted; on the other, President Roosevelt had told him that Britain and America would only contribute naval and air forces to an international coercion operation, i.e. weapons with a momentary effect, whilst Soviet and Chinese land forces would provide the occupation forces. The least one can say is that from then on the Kremlin had particular views on the future of Chiang Kai-shek's China.

Similarly, there would only be advantages for Stalin if he unreservedly accepted another suggestion of Roosevelt's, according to which, when peace was restored, Japan's bases for aggression in the Pacific islands would be handed over to the United Nations administration, in fact to the "four policemen". He even proposed to apply the same statute at Dakar, and if Britain agreed to hand over Singapore and Hong Kong to the International organisation, she could perhaps be given certain territorial advantages elsewhere, particularly, he thought, at the expense of Spain, who would be invited to give up to Britain a zone of her territory adjacent to Gibraltar.

The American historian Robert E. Sherwood attributes this singular proposition to Stalin's continual teasing of his British ally, with Roosevelt an amused conciliator. But one could also see, under a bantering disguise, an attempt to sound the British out, to which there was no response . . .

Mass executions?

In any event–teasing or no teasing–the dinner of November 30 which brought the three delegations together was the occasion of an outburst from Churchill when Stalin, in the same humorous tone, mentioned how convenient it would be to have 50,000 German officers and military technicians shot the better to assure the peace of the world. When he heard this, the Prime Minister replied energetically:

"The British Parliament and public will never tolerate mass executions. Even if in war passion they allow them to begin they would turn violently against those responsible after the first butchery had taken place. The Soviets must be under no delusion on this point."

And when Stalin returned to the idea, he added in an even more high-minded manner:

"I would rather be taken out into the garden here and now and be shot myself than sully my own and my country's honour by such infamy."

The American president tried to cool the atmosphere by suggesting that they restrict themselves to shooting 49,000, but this joke did not have the intended effect and when his son, Colonel Elliot Roosevelt, had allowed himself an unseemly toast associating the U.S. Army with Stalin's wish, Churchill left the room and slammed the door behind him.

Naturally Stalin, together with Molotov, rushed after him and at length reassured him by telling him that there was nothing serious in his remarks. But in his memoirs, Churchill maintains that these explanations had not for a moment convinced him "completely" and looking back, his opinion had not changed. In our opinion, this meant that Stalin, when he made suggestions which were out of tune with the normal convivial atmosphere at a banquet, wanted to find out what the reaction of his table companions would be to the systematic extermination of the German officer corps. But from the fact that Churchill lost his temper at the idea that Stalin would make use of his name to justify such an outrage, we are entitled to conclude that even then he had no doubt that Stalin was entirely responsible for the Katyn massacre.

Given the "compromise" suggested as a joke by Roosevelt, we must on the other hand conclude that he believed or wanted to believe in the Russians' innocence in the Katyn affair. In fact he had never been more optimistic, not only regarding the outcome of World War II, but also the future of international relations. The Soviet Union had, after all, through its first representative adhered to his idea of

△ △ General Wladyslaw Sikorski, Premier of the Polish government-in-exile. He was killed in an air crash on July 4 1943.

△ His successor Stanislas Mikolajczyk. Relations between the Poles and the Russians broke down after the Katyn disclosures.

▲ *General Dwight D. Eisenhower. He was promoted to command the Allied invasion force for operation "Overlord", a move which was politically expedient, but which disappointed Brooke, who had been promised the command by Churchill.*

▼ *General Sir Henry Maitland Wilson, who succeeded Eisenhower as Supreme Allied Commander in the Mediterranean theatre of operations.*

the United Nations as well as the "four policemen" system.

The note taken by Lord Moran after this short outburst, confided to him by Churchill but not mentioned in his memoirs, may be regarded as evidence. After the session during which the agreement between the British and American Chiefs-of-Staff and Marshal Voroshilov on the war plans for 1944 was settled, the Prime Minister, for form's sake, put this question to Harry Hopkins:

" 'Tell me, Harry, is the President quite certain about Moscow?'

" 'Why, sure,' answered Hopkins. 'The President knows now that Stalin is "getatable" and that we are going to get along fine in the future.' "

The consequences are well known, but it would be incorrect to dissociate Teheran from Yalta and Potsdam. Those who have done so have unconsciously given in to their wish to play down the British responsibility and particularly Churchill's for the catastrophes that followed, the consequences of which we still suffer. Admitting that this responsibility is not so heavy as Roosevelt's and Hopkins's, it still exists, since the arrangements made at Potsdam and Yalta were the inevitable consequences of the Teheran decisions.

As a result of this conference, Lord Mountbatten received notice that he could not for the time being rely on any increase in landing craft; this meant that Operation "Buccaneer" was postponed to a more favourable time, if not indefinitely. And General Stilwell, who had remained in Cairo, was charged with the unpleasant task of informing Chiang Kaishek.

Eisenhower chosen for "Overlord"

In the meantime President Roosevelt finally gave in to those of his advisers who were persuading him not to release General Marshall, who was rightly considered to be indispensable at the summit of the American military hierarchy. On his way back he summoned General Eisenhower to Tunis, and as soon as Eisenhower had joined him in his car, he said: "Well, Ike, you are going to command 'Overlord'." Eisenhower replied:

"Mr President, I realize that such an appointment involved difficult decisions. I hope you will not be disappointed."

"On Christmas Eve we listened to the radio, having learned that President Roosevelt was to make a significant speech. During that talk he made the first public announcement of my transfer to command of OVERLORD and included in the statement the designation of the title I was to assume. The title was Supreme Commander, Allied Expeditionary Forces. This sounded very imposing and inspired Commander Butcher, my naval aide, to say that his major problem for the next week would be to design proper stationery to carry my exalted title."

The post of C.-in-C. Allied Forces in the Mediterranean then became vacant. General Sir Henry Maitland Wilson ("Jumbo" Wilson) was appointed by agreement between Brooke and Marshall; the C.I.G.S. then appointed General Sir Bernard Paget to the command of the British Forces in the Middle East.

CHAPTER 106

Smashing the Dniepr front

The first five months of 1944 were marked by new Red Army offensives to the south of the Pripet Marshes. The offensives led to the liberation of the Ukraine and Crimea as well as to the conquest of the northern part of Rumanian Moldavia, while in the Leningrad region they succeeded in throwing the Germans back from a line linking Oranienbaum–Volkhov–Novgorod–Lake Ilmen onto one linking Narva–Lake Peipus and Pskov. At the same time, the Western Allies were also putting the pressure on Germany.

Further south, General Sir Henry Maitland Wilson, new Allied Commander-in-Chief in the Mediterranean, endeavoured to carry out the limited mission which had been entrusted to him in implementation of decisions recently taken at the Teheran Conference. Two days before the Normandy landings, the advance guard of his 15th Army Group had entered Rome hard on the enemy's heels. Thereby General Alexander had achieved his strictly geographical objective, but arguably at the price of sacrificing his strategic objective, namely the destruction of the enemy forces. This is a question to which we shall return later.

Parallel to this, in Great Britain the preparations for Operation "Overlord", with all their attendant difficulties, were rapidly approaching their climax. While the divisions taking part in the landings by sea and by air were undergoing intensive training, in London Generals Eisenhower and Montgomery were putting the final touches to the invasion plans drawn up by the American and British Combined Chiefs-of-Staff, C.O.S.S.A.C., and submitted for their approval by General Morgan.

Bombing stepped up

Anglo-American bomber formations intensified their missions by day and by night over the Third Reich as well as over occupied Europe. Most probably the results obtained over the first six months were no more significant in their impact on German war production than during the previous year. However, systematic pinpointing of synthetic oil plants from spring onwards, as well as of the Ploiești oil-wells, enabled the Allied air forces for the first time to influence events on land directly by precipitating an extremely serious fuel crisis in the Wehrmacht. Furthermore, in the western and southern theatres British and American fighter-bombers and medium bombers constantly pounded the enemy's communications

▽ "Crush the Fascist Reptile!" A typically virulent Russian poster. In the early days of the war, when they were exhibited near the front line, posters served to demoralise the attacking Germans in addition to whipping the Russians into greater hatred of the invaders.

▷ *U-boats of the excellent XXI type under construction in a Bremen yard at the time of Germany's capitulation.*

system. In France and Belgium their aim was to obstruct rapid reinforcement of the German 7th Army, which was in position on the coast between Cabourg and St. Nazaire; in Italy their main targets were the Po bridges and the course of the Adige, the route by which enemy supplies and reinforcements moved after crossing the Brenner Pass.

War in the Atlantic

On June 22, 1941, Hitler became involved unwisely in a "war on two fronts" such as had cost Wilhelm II his throne, in spite of the fact that the Emperor's ghost might have seemed to have been exorcised by the Soviet-German Pact of August 23, 1939. And now on January 1, 1944, the Third Reich and its Führer were in a position of having to conduct a "war on all fronts" (*Allfrontenkrieg*), as Professor Percy Ernst Schramm (who at the time was responsible for the O.K.W. war diary) has put it.

The only way in which Germany might have escaped the inevitable consequences of the powerful efforts of the Allies to surround and close in on her, would have been to resume the U-boat offensive in the Atlantic with the same success as in 1942. But for all his energy, intelligence, and experience, Grand-Admiral Dönitz was unable to stem the swelling tide of troops, war *matériel,* and supplies converging on Europe from America.

The facts are made clear in the following table, based on figures supplied by Captain Roskill, of Allied mercantile losses in 1942 and 1944:

	1942		*1944*	
	tonnage	*ships*	*tonnage*	*ships*
January	276,795	48	36,065	5
February	429,891	73	12,577	2
March	534,064	95	36,867	7
April	391,044	66	34,224	5
May	576,350	120	0	0
Totals	2,208,144	402	119,733	19

The figures show the extent to which Britain and America recovered complete supremacy in the North Atlantic, with consequent complete freedom of manoeuvre and strategy. Most probably Grand-Admiral Dönitz was keeping new and unpleasant secret weapons up his sleeve, but they were not as yet ready, and until they were there was a great deal that could happen.

Hitler's predictions

The immediate consequences of this complete reversal of the situation were perfectly clear to Hitler. One only need refer to the arguments propounded on November 3, 1943 in support of measures prescribed by his Directive No. 51, as regards the conduct of the war; in his own words:

"The hard and costly struggle against Bolshevism during the last two-and-a-half years, which has involved the bulk of our military strength in the East, has demanded extreme exertions. The greatness of the danger and the general situation demanded it. But the situation has since changed. The danger in the East still remains, but a greater danger now appears in the West: an Anglo-Saxon landing! In the East, the vast extent of the territory makes it possible for us to lose ground, even on a large scale, without a fatal blow being dealt to the nervous system of Germany.

"It is very different in the West! Should the enemy succeed in breaching our defences on a wide front here, the immediate consequences would be unpredictable. Everything indicates that the enemy will launch an offensive against the Western front of Europe, at the latest in the spring, perhaps even earlier.

"I can therefore no longer take responsibility for further weakening the West, in favour of other theatres of war. I have therefore decided to reinforce its defences, particularly those places from which the long-range bombardment of England will begin. For it is here that the enemy must and will attack, and it is here–unless all indications are misleading–that the decisive battle against the landing forces will be fought."

On December 20 following, Hitler returned to the question in the presence of his generals. It appears from the shorthand account of his statement that, while he was convinced that the invasion would take place, he was less than convinced that the British would have their hearts in it:

"It stands to reason that the English have less confidence in this enterprise than has Eisenhower. Eisenhower has effected one [*sic*] successful invasion, but this was solely due to the work of traitors. Here with our soldiers he will find none to help him. Here, we mean business, make no mistake! It is a totally different matter to invade North Africa and be greeted by Monsieur Giraud or be confronted by the Italians who for the most part stay in their holes without firing a single shot, and to set foot in the West in the face of unrelenting fire. And so long as a battery is capable of firing, it will continue firing. That is a certainty."

German misconceptions

The above extract from Directive No. 51 is interesting from more than one aspect. Its third paragraph adds a further reason to those normally advanced by way of explaining why O.K.W. situated the centre of gravity of its western defensive system between Le Havre and the Pas-de-Calais. The argument at Rastenburg ran as follows: the fact that the launching sites for the V-1 and V-2, whose effect was directed against Britain, were in this area would in all probability lead the British to urge their allies that this was the best place to make the landings. This argument was plausible enough, but its effectiveness required one condition,

▽ *Evidence of the Red Air Force's growing power–German transport destroyed during the retreat in the Ukraine. From now on the Luftwaffe could only very rarely assure the ground forces of any useful air cover.*

▵ *German and satellite infantry wait to board a train leaving for the Russian front.*

namely that the Germans should be the first to open fire. Yet Hitler knew perfectly well that the V-1 missiles (let alone V-2) would not be operational before the date when he expected his enemies to attempt invasion across the Channel.

Furthermore, insisting as he did on the peril that was looming in the West to the extent of giving it priority in the short run over the Soviet threat, Hitler's judgement was correct. On the basis of this eminently reasonable view of the situation, seen from the perspective of O.K.W., Hitler went on to deduce that the Anglo-American attempt at invasion would fail so long as he did not, as he had done during the winters of 1941–2 and 1942–3, prop up the now tottering Eastern Front with troops from among those guarding the Atlantic battlements.

Thence it follows that he to whom the directive of November 3, 1943 was principally addressed, that is Hitler himself, this time in his capacity as commander-in-chief of German land forces, would draw the logical conclusions from the premises he had just himself stated in his office at Rastenburg.

At O.K.H., Colonel-General Zeitzler perhaps flattered himself for several weeks that he would be given more freedom of action than hitherto in the conduct of operations. Was it not there in writing, in Hitler's own hand, that if it were a case of absolute necessity on the Eastern Front, withdrawals on a fairly considerable scale could be countenanced without necessarily putting the "nervous system" of the Third Reich in mortal danger?

The Führer and Russia

But when it came down to it, the Russians' third winter offensive, the Führer showed the same persistent and mistaken obstinacy as he had done in the previous years, bringing his familiar arguments of high politics and the war economy to bear against his army group commanders every time one of them sought to advise him of a suitable chance to disengage in the face of the sheer weight, regardless of cost, of the Soviet onslaught.

And evidence of this came with the fresh disasters that occurred, principally to the south of the Pripet Marshes, when towards the end of January 1944 Kanev and Korsun' and, on the following May 13, Sevastopol' found their doleful place in the annals of German military history. So it was again a case of immediately arresting the possible consequences of these new defeats sustained by the Third Reich and, since the few reinforcements still available on the Eastern Front were quite inadequate, Hitler the head of O.K.H. sought help from Hitler the head of O.K.W. in order to avert imminent catastrophe. In these circumstances, born of his quite inexcusable obstinacy, Hitler the supreme commander had no alternative but to depart from the principle he had laid down in his Directive of November 3, 1943. At the end of the winter of 1943, the *Waffen*-S.S. II Panzer Corps had to be transferred from the Alençon sector, and hence missed the rendezvous of June 6, 1944 in Normandy.

Manstein's impossible task

The Soviet winter offensive began on December 24, 1943 on either side of the Kiev-Zhitomir road and within a few weeks involved the whole of Army Group "South" which, at that time, stretching as it did between the estuary of the Dniepr and the Mozyr' region, comprised the 6th Army (General Hollidt), the 1st *Panzerarmee* (General Hube), the 8th Army (General Wöhler), and the 4th *Panzerarmee* (General Raus). The entire group, commanded as before by Field-Marshal Erich von Manstein, was made up of 73 of the 180 divisions that were then engaged in the battle between Kerch' Strait and the Oranienbaum bridgehead on the Baltic.

In particular, 22 of the 32 Panzer and *Panzergrenadier* divisions on the Eastern Front were allocated to Army Group "South".

The 18th Artillery Division had also been assigned there, with its eight tracked or motorised battalions, comprising nine 21-cm howitzers, plus 30 15-cm, 48 10.5-cm, and 12 10-cm guns. This was a new formation, based on similar ones in the Red Army, and much was expected of it. But it proved disappointing and was disbanded after a few months. A total of 73 divisions seems impressive, but the figure is misleading. Between July 31, 1943 and July 31, 1944, Manstein lost 405,409 killed, wounded, and missing, yet in the same period his reinforcements in officers, N.C.O.s, and other ranks amounted to only 221,893. His divisions, particularly the infantry ones, were thin on the ground. It was the same story with the Panzer divisions, which in spite of increased production of tanks, were 50 to 60 per cent below complement. And the front to be defended, in the Führer's words "with no thought of retreat", measured a good 650 miles.

4th *Panzerarmee* defeated

As has been noted, the 1st Ukrainian Front (General N. F. Vatutin) inaugurated the Soviet winter offensive on December 24. With fire support from four artillery divisions and ten artillery regiments (936 guns and howitzers) assigned from general reserve, Vatutin launched an attack on an 18-mile front in the direction of Zhitomir, with 18 divisions (38th Army and 1st Guards Army) backed by six armoured or mechanised corps. The XXIV Panzer Corps (General Nehring: 8th and 19th Panzer

△ *Colonel-General P. S. Rybalko, twice a "Hero of the Soviet Union", was one of Stalin's most able and respected tank generals.*

▽ *A German 15-cm gun battery on the move on one of Russia's better roads. With the already efficient Russian artillery growing ever stronger, German artillery now found itself in very dire straits.*
Overleaf: *Russian infantry move in to dislodge the Germans from a village they are holding.*

Divisions and *Waffen*-S.S. 2nd Panzer Division *"Das Reich"*) put up a stubborn resistance for 48 hours, then, in spite of being reinforced by XLVIII Panzer Corps (General Balck) broke under the impact. The 3rd Guards Tank Army (General Rybalko) stormed through the breach and on the last day of the year recaptured Zhitomir and by January 3 reached Novograd-Volinskiy, over 85 miles from its jumping-off point. Further to the right, the Soviet 60th and 13th Armies, comprising 14 infantry divisions, had retaken Korosten and were close to the Russo-Polish frontier of the Treaty of Riga; on Rybalko's left, Vatutin's centre was overwhelming the defenders of Berdichev.

Hence the defeat of the 4th *Panzerarmee* took on a strategic dimension, and in the event of Vatutin exploiting his success to the south-west resolutely and with vigour, could have led to the total destruction of Army Groups "South" and "A". As early as December 25, Manstein had been aware of the possibility of such a danger and had alerted O.K.H. to this effect, confronting it with the following dilemma: "The 4th Army was no longer capable of defending the flank of Army Groups 'South' and 'A'; effective reinforcements were vital. If O.K.H. was unable to provide these, we would be obliged to take five or six divisions at least from our right wing, which clearly could not then maintain its positions inside the Dniepr loop. We sought our liberty of movement for that wing."

Manstein was certainly not taken in by the expedient to which Hitler had recourse in these circumstances, when the latter requested further information. Even so, at the time when he was writing his memoirs, Manstein had no knowledge of the disobliging, indeed absurd, comments that his report had drawn from the Führer: that Manstein had inflated the enemy numbers knowingly in the hope of imposing his personal decisions on O.K.H. Furthermore, the troops were bound to mirror their commander's attitude, and if some divisions failed to measure up to the standards needed, it was because Manstein, lacking in conviction, had failed to galvanise them with the necessary determination.

Hitler went on, in the presence of Zeitzler, who must have been somewhat dumbfounded, about the heroic times when the party assumed power, capturing in turn Mecklenburg, East Prussia ("refractory and reactionary"), Cologne ("red

▵ *A small party of Germans pulls back past the wreckage of a shot-up motor convoy.*
▹ *"Dniepropetrovsk is ours!" thunders this Kukryniksy cartoon of the "Bandit of Melitopol" being driven back out of Russia.*

and black"), and–according to the stenographic account of the meeting–"Thuringia was dyed a deep red, but then I had a Koch at the time I wanted him, at another time a Ley or a Sauckel. There were men for you. When, by some mischance, I didn't have the right men at hand, there was trouble. I took it as axiomatic that good *Gaus* made good *Gauleiters*. And it's not a jot different today."

Manstein pleads for reinforcements . . .

In any case, whatever the parallel between the situation of the Nazi Party in its electoral campaigns and the Russian campaign, Manstein, who had been offered two or three divisions by Hitler with which to plug the two breaches, each 45 to 50 miles in width, to right and left of the 4th *Panzerarmee,* proceeded on December 29 to carry out the manoeuvre he had proposed in his report of December 25. The 1st *Panzerarmee* command "castled" from right to left of the 8th Army, transferring III Panzer Corps (General Breith) with its four divisions from the Dniepr loop and completing the movement by shifting VII Corps and XXIV Panzer Corps, which formed Raus's right flank, to the south-east of Berdichev. This manoeuvre, which was approved by O.K.H., provided some relief for Army Group "South", added to the fact that Vatutin failed to exploit his opportunity to drive to the Dniestr from Kamenets-Podolskiy. Hitler, however, had not let pass without response Manstein's proposal to evacuate the Dniepr loop and the Nikopol' bridgehead. It so happened that on January 3, General Konev himself launched an attack in the Kirovograd sector, where the German 6th Army had just relieved the completely exhausted 1st *Panzerarmee.*

. . . and tries to convince Hitler

A clear decision was called for and with the object of obtaining one, Manstein went to Rastenburg in person, hoping that he would carry more weight with the Führer than his teletype messages. He put his case as follows:

"If the high command could not bring up strong reinforcements immediately, our Southern wing would have to fall back, abandoning Nikopol', and hence the Crimea, simply in order to make good the deficiency; and this in our opinion was only a first step. We had reconnoitred positions in the rear and given orders for their preparation. These positions more or less followed the course of the Bug, making use of any high ground that seemed advantageous, up to a point south of the sector where our Northern wing

△ *Maintenance work in progress on a Büssing-NAG SWS heavy gun tractor fitted with a ten-barrel 15-cm* Nebelwerfer *battery.*

was at the moment engaged in fighting. Occupation of these new positions would reduce the 600 mile front by almost half, held too thinly by the 6th and 8th Armies. Such a drastic reduction, and the availability of the 17th Army once it was withdrawn from Crimea, would enable us to achieve the degree of consolidation required in the Northern wing."

And anticipating the likely objection of the Führer, he added: "Naturally the Russians would also benefit by the operation, but since our front would thereby achieve greater solidity, its defensive capacity would be enhanced–and this is the greatest asset in war–so as to be able to resist even massive assault. Furthermore, the destruction of the railway system would prevent the enemy moving the forces now available to him with sufficient speed to allow him to maintain his superiority to west of Kiev."

Hitler stubbornly opposed the propositions made to him in these terms. The need for Nikopol' manganese, whose mining had been suspended for several weeks, prohibited him from abandoning the Dniepr loop. And as for evacuating the Crimea, the idea should be totally excluded; it could well bring about the defection of Bulgaria and a declaration of war on Germany by Turkey. Nor was there any question of finding reinforcements from Army Group "North": if Field-Marshal von Küchler was forced to abandon his positions dominating the Gulf of Finland, Russian submarines would operate freely in the Baltic and cut the supply lines for Swedish iron-ore between Luleå and factories in Germany.

Manstein returned, disabused and empty-handed, to his H.Q. at Vinnitsa. From one of his several meetings with Hitler, the Field-Marshal took away the following impression of the dictator's face gripped, as was then the case, with inner fury:

"I saw Hitler's features harden. He threw me a glance which signified 'there is no further argument'. I cannot remember ever in my life having seen anyone portray such force of character. One of the foreign ambassadors accredited to Berlin speaks in his memoirs of the effect produced on him by Hitler's eyes. Alone in a coarse and undistinguished face they constituted the single striking feature, certainly the only expressive one. Those eyes fixed me as if they would annihilate me. The comparison with a Hindu snake-charmer suddenly struck me. For the space of a few seconds a kind of mute struggle took place between us. That gaze told me how he had contrived to dominate so many people."

The intervention of the 1st *Panzerarmee*, under the command of the gallant General Hube, may have allowed Manstein both to contain the centre of the 1st Ukrainian Front and even make it give ground a little after sustaining heavy casualties (during the second half of January on the furious Pogrebishche sector), but General Raus's northern wing, which presented a ragged line northwards to the Pripet Marshes, proved unable to resist the pressure applied on it by General Vatutin's right wing. On the previous January 4, in the course of his visit to O.K.H., Manstein had urged Hitler to build up a strong reserve in the Rovno region. His advice had not been followed, and this important fortress-town fell to the Russians on February 5, 1944. Since its breakthrough on December 24, the 1st Ukrainian Front had thus far advanced 170 miles westwards, with the result that the line Army Group "South" was required to hold was vastly lengthened from its furthest point at Nikopol', without receiving proportionate reinforcement. Also, lines of communication were increasingly under threat to the extent that the Russians exploited their gains in the direction of Ternopol', only 90 miles to the south of Rovno.

Dangerous salient

In the immediate future, the situation was still more serious. On Hitler's express orders, the right of the 1st *Panzerarmee* and the left of the 8th Army were maintained on the banks of the Dniepr between Kanev and upstream of Cherkassy. With Vatutin's advance as far as Zhachkov and with Konev in possession of Kirovograd on January 10 a dangerous salient 100 miles wide and some 90 miles deep had formed in this sector, which gave the enemy the opportunity for a pincer movement. The reduction of the front (on the lines proposed to the Führer by Manstein at their meeting on January 4 at Rastenburg, a course which he continued to advocate in notes and personal letters) brooked no further argument; and subsequent events show that the whole manoeuvre, delicate though it was, might well have succeeded with the least cost; reckoning from January 4, there was an effective delay of three weeks, while the 1st and 2nd Ukrainian Fronts together cut off the area between Kanev and Cherkassy; of almost four weeks before the 3rd Ukrainian Front (under General Malinovsky) attacked the Nikopol' bridgehead; and of nearly five weeks before General Vatutin's armoured and mechanised advanced units reached the Rovno–Shepetovka line.

The weather takes a hand

Soviet commentators attribute the relatively slow progress of the Russians to the constant changes in temperature and alternation of rain and snow recorded in the west of the Ukraine during the months of January and February 1944.

Writing in 1956, Colonel A. N. Grylev of the Soviet Army has this to say:

"Unfavourable weather conditions created more difficulties for our troops than did the crossing of rivers. An unusually early spring caused the snow to melt as early as the end of January. Rain and melting snow aggravated the difficulties. Rivers overflowed their banks. Roads and tracks became as impracticable for vehicles as was the terrain for infantry. These various factors had a considerable effect on our military activities, limiting the possibility of manoeuvre and hampering supplies of food, fuel, and munitions."

Lest it should be felt that the writer is trying to excuse the purely relative failure of the Soviet armies to annihilate the German army groups facing the four Ukrainian Fronts, Colonel Grylev's testimony is borne out in detail by General

▽ *Hungarian artillerymen move a somewhat antiquated piece of field artillery into position.*

△ *A Russian poster extols the Red Air Force, now master of the skies over Russia.*

von Vormann, who was in the same area as commander of the hard-pressed XLVII Panzer Corps:

"The *rasputitsa* (thaw) had set in astonishingly early; everywhere it is spring mud . . . Worked on by the sun, the rain, and the warm winds, the heavy, black Ukraine earth turns into thick sticky mud during the day. There is not one metalled road in the country. On foot you sink down to your shins and after a few steps lose shoes and socks there. Wheeled vehicles stall and get stuck. Suction by the mud tore away the too-narrow tracks of our all-purpose transports. The only machines capable of making any headway were the tractors and the tanks, which rolled their way forwards at a maximum speed of 3 miles an hour but at the cost of tremendous strain on the engine and huge petrol consumption."

At all events, it is clear that the mud worked more to the disadvantage of the Russians than of the Germans, since in their task of attack and pursuit they also had to cope with the battlefield debris left by the retreating enemy, who destroyed everything of any value behind him.

Manstein a defeatist?

In Manstein's dispute with Hitler, are there grounds for accusing the former–as has been alleged from time to time–of having been obsessed with withdrawal in the face of any build-up in enemy strength or else of having been unjustifiably alarmed by the spectre of encirclement?

It is clear that at this juncture Manstein no longer displayed the genius for bold moves that had characterised his performance between 1941 and 1943; yet it is also abundantly clear that he was no longer in a position where he could act boldly. Apart from XLVI Panzer Corps, which had recently been assigned to him, he knew that he could expect no further reinforcements from the west and that on the Eastern Front it was a case of robbing Peter to pay Paul. The liquidation of a pocket containing half a dozen divisions would mean not only the loss of some 60,000 men and most of their *matériel,* but, further, a breach of 75 to 90 miles in his now dangerously reduced defensive system. The battle of Korsun'-Shevchen-

▽ *Soviet artillery batters away at the German positions near Leningrad.*

kovskiy would show that his appreciation of the situation–and he had vainly tried to prevail on Hitler to accept it–was the correct one.

On January 25, Marshal Zhukov, who had been delegated by *Stavka* to co-ordinate operations, threw the troops of the 1st and 2nd Ukrainian Fronts into an assault on the Kanev salient. General Vatutin brought his 40th Army (Lieutenant-General E. F. Zhmachenko) and 27th Army (Lieutenant-General S. G. Trofimenko) to bear on the western front of the salient. They had a considerable job in overcoming German resistance so as to open a breach for brigades of the 6th Tank Army (Lieutenant-General A. G. Kravchenko) to move south-eastwards. The 2nd Ukrainian Front, under General Konev, seems to have had an easier task; delivering its attack at the point of junction of XLVII Panzer Corps and XI Corps, the 4th Guards Army (Major-General A. I. Ryzhov) and 53rd Army (Major-General I. V. Galanin) swiftly broke through the lines held by the 389th Infantry Division, thus enabling the 5th Guards Tank Army, under the command of General P. A. Rotmistrov, to be unleashed without further ado.

"There could be no other adequate analogy. The sea-dikes had given and the tide, interminable and vast, spread across the plain, passing either side of our tanks which, with packets of infantry round them, had the appearance of reefs rising from the swell. Our amazement was at its peak when in the afternoon cavalry units, galloping westwards, broke through our screen of fire in close formation. It was a sight long-forgotten, almost a mirage–V Guards Cavalry Corps, with the 11th, 12th, and 63rd Cavalry Divisions under the command of Selimanov." Thus, in a monograph dealing with this episode, the former commander of XLVII Panzer Corps describes the breakthrough at Krasnosilka (30 miles north-west of Kirovograd). In these conditions, it is not surprising that Vatutin's and Konev's tanks effected a meeting on January 28 in the region of Zvenigorodka. XI Corps, which formed the left of the German 8th Army, and XLII Corps, on the right of the 1st *Panzerarmee,* were caught in the trap along with four infantry divisions (the 57th, 72nd, 88th, and 389th), the 5th S.S. *Panzergrenadier* Division *"Wiking"* and the S.S. *Freiwilligen Sturmbrigade "Wallonie"*, which Himmler had recruited in the French-speaking provinces of Belgium. By virtue of seniority over his comrade Lieutenant-General T. Lieb, General W. Stemmermann, commander of XI Corps, assumed command of those encircled.

Hitler hangs on to Kanev

Hitler was determined to defend the Kanev salient at all costs, as he considered it the base for launching an offensive which would force the Russians to cross back over the Dniepr in the region of Kiev. Hence orders were given to Stemmermann to hold his positions and to establish himself so as to be able to repulse any attacks from the south; to General O. Wöhler, commanding the 8th Army, to hurl his XLVII Panzer Corps, reinforced to a strength of five Panzer divisions, at the eastern face of the pocket; and to General H. V. Hube, to drive his III Panzer Corps, comprising four Panzer divisions (among them the 1st S.S. Panzer Division *"Leibstandarte Adolf Hitler"*) at the western face of the pocket.

Such a plan, involving the concentration of nine Panzer divisions against the Kanev pocket, was nevertheless doomed to failure within the time limit imposed by the defenders' capacity to hold out, though an airlift was being organised to keep them in supplies. Moreover, most of the Panzer divisions designated by Hitler were already engaged elsewhere, and hence it was a case of relieving them, pulling them out of line, and moving them to their jump-off

△ *Russian peasant women greet the arrival of liberating Soviet armour, complete with tank-riders.*

△ *Not all the Russians welcomed the Red Army as liberators, however, and many, particularly from the western regions, fell back with the retreating Germans.*

points. Furthermore, they were far short of complement; in particular their grenadier regiments were reduced to only several hundred rifles, and there were grounds for feeling some apprehension that they lacked the resilience necessary for a rapid thrust. Yet in counter-attacks speed is all.

Indeed, on February 2, XLVII and III Panzer Corps still had only four Panzer divisions and, what is more, one of them was immediately withdrawn from General N. von Vormann's XLVII Panzer Corps by special order of the Führer, on receipt of the news that units of the 3rd Ukrainian Front were advancing on Apostolovo, which lies half-way between Nikopol' and Krivoy-Rog. The following night, the *rasputitsa* arrived, covering the western Ukraine with the sea of mud described above. Now the unseasonable weather worked to the advantage of the Russians, delaying their enemy's movements still further. When the earth grew hard again, around February 10, the Soviet encirclement of the Korsun' pocket was consolidated to such an extent that III Panzer Corps only managed to reach the area of Lysyanka, eight miles from the lines held by the besieged forces.

Break-out attempt

General Stemmermann, as one might expect, had not succeeded in forming a front to the south as he had been enjoined to do in his orders from Rastenburg, without at the same time abandoning Kanev and the banks of the Dniepr, which would have been in defiance of these orders. On February 8 he gave no reply to a summons to capitulate transmitted to him from General Konev, under orders to reduce the pocket. Both Stemmermann and his subordinates turned a deaf ear to the exhortations made to them by representatives of the "Committee for a Free Germany" who had been conveyed to the battlefield on Moscow's orders and were led by General von

Seydlitz-Kurzbach, former commander of LI Corps, who had been taken prisoner at Stalingrad. The tracts and individual free passes scattered among the soldiers with a view to encouraging surrender were equally ignored.

Notwithstanding, the airlift worked poorly in the face of an abundant and highly effective Soviet fighter force, and those encircled at Korsun' saw their strength diminish further each day. It was inevitable that the order should come to attempt to break out towards III Panzer Corps, which had been conclusively halted by the mud. It was the only chance left.

To this effect, General Stemmermann reassembled the remnants of his two corps round the village of Shanderovka and organised them in three echelons: at the head the grenadiers, bayonets fixed, next the heavy infantry units, and then finally the artillery and service troops. The 57th and 88th Infantry Divisions protected the rear and showed themselves equal to the sacrifice they were called upon to give. The attempt took place in the night of February 16–17, but at first light Soviet artillery, tanks, and aircraft were able to react with vigour and immediate effect:

"Till now," writes General von Vormann, "our forces had dragged all their heavy equipment across gullies filled with thick, impacted snow. But then enemy shelling proved our undoing. Artillery and assault guns were abandoned after they had exhausted their ammunition. And then the wounded moving with the troops met their fate . . . Veritable hordes of hundreds of soldiers from every type of unit headed westwards under the nearest available officer. The enemy infantry were swept out of the way by our advancing bayonets; even the tanks turned in their tracks. But all the same Russian fire struck with impunity at the masses, moving forward with heads down, unevenly and unprotected. Our losses multiplied . . . "

This hopeless charge by 40,000 men foundered on the natural obstacle of the Gniloy-Tikich, a stream which had thawed only a few days previously, and was now 25 feet wide and just deep enough for a man to drown in. And it heralded a fresh disaster, which the Belgian Léon Degrelle, fighting in the ranks of the S.S. *Sturmbrigade "Wallonie"*, describes in unforgettable terms:

"The artillery teams which had escaped destruction plunged first into the waves and ice floes. The banks of the river were steep, the horses turned back and were drowned. Men then threw themselves in to cross the river by swimming. But hardly had they got to the other side than they were transformed into blocks of ice, and their clothes frozen to their bodies. They tried to throw their equipment over the river. But often their uniforms fell into the current. Soon hundreds of soldiers, completely naked and red as lobsters, were thronging the other bank. Many soldiers did not know how to swim. Maddened by the approach of the Russian armour which was coming down the slope and firing at them, they threw themselves pell-mell into the icy water. Some escaped death by clinging to trees which had been hastily felled . . . but hundreds were drowned. Under the fire of tanks thousands upon thousands of soldiers, half clothed, streaming with icy water or naked as the day they were born, ran through the snow towards the distant cottages of Lysyanka."

△ *By the beginning of 1944 the "Nazi Victory Express" had not only been halted but pushed firmly into reverse by Stalin's "adjustments" to the line.*

▽ *A German assessment of Russian thinking: "Be careful, comrades! The Germans are bandits, and the Americans gangsters. But worst of all are the British: they're our allies!"*

▵ *Part of the German bag taken in the Korsun'-Shevchenkovskiy pocket.*

The hecatomb of Lysyanka

In short, between February 16 and 18, III Panzer Corps at Lysyanka retrieved only 30,000 survivors, unarmed for the most part; among them, General Lieb, commander of XLII Corps. The valiant Stemmermann had been killed by a piece of shrapnel. According to the Soviet historian B. S. Telpukhovsky, of the Moscow Academy of Sciences, on this one occasion the Russians accounted for more than 52,000 dead and 11,000 prisoners but his German colleagues Hillgruber and Jacobsen take issue with him: "Just before the investment occurred the two German corps numbered 54,000 all told, including rear area troops, some of whom escaped encirclement."

Allowing for the 30,000 or 32,000 survivors of this 21-day tragedy, German losses in the sector could barely have risen to more than one third of the total claimed by Moscow nearly 15 years after Germany's unconditional surrender. Hillgruber's and Jacobsen's figures are beyond question.

Alexander Werth quotes the account of a Soviet eye witness of these tragic events which confirms General von Vormann's account. On the day following, Major Kampov told Werth:

"I remember that last fateful night of the 17th of February. A terrible blizzard was blowing. Konev himself was travelling in a tank through the shell-shattered 'corridor'. I rode on horseback from one point in the corridor to another, with a dispatch from the General; it was so dark that I could not see the horse's ears. I mention this darkness and this blizzard because they are an important factor in what happened . . .

"It was during that night, or the evening before, that the encircled Germans, having abandoned all hope of ever being rescued by Hube, decided to make a last desperate effort to break out . . .

"Driven out of their warm huts they had to abandon Shanderovka. They flocked into the ravines near the village, and then took the desperate decision to break through early in the morning . . . So that morning they formed themselves into two marching columns of about 14,000 each . . .

"It was about six o'clock in the morning. Our tanks and our cavalry suddenly appeared and rushed straight into the thick of the two columns. What happened then is hard to describe. The Germans ran in all directions. And for the next four hours our tanks raced up and down the plain crushing them by the hundred. Our cavalry, competing with the tanks, chased them through the ravines where it was hard for the tanks to pursue them. Most of the time the tanks were not using their guns lest they hit their own cavalry. Hundreds and hundreds of cavalry were hacking at them with their sabres, and massacred the Fritzes as no one had ever been massacred by cavalry before. There was no time to take prisoners. It was the kind of carnage that nothing could stop till it was all over. In a small area over 20,000 Germans were killed."

In connection with this episode, General von Vormann, in the study mentioned above, raises an interesting question. Observing that the encirclement of XI and XLII Corps on January 28 had opened a 65-mile breach between the right of III Panzer Corps and the left of XLVII, he considers why the Soviet high command failed to exploit the opportunity of a breakthrough afforded. In his opinion, on that day there was nothing to prevent Stalin driving his armoured units towards Uman' and across the Bug, assigning to them distant objectives on the Dniestr, the Prut, and in the Rumanian Carpathians. This not impossible objective would have sealed the fate of Army Groups "A" and "South".

This question was raised in 1954, but it is still impossible to provide an answer which documents can verify. We must be content with the supposition that Stalin acted with extreme prudence, by annihilating the Korsun' pocket before embarking on more hazardous enterprises, and it should be noted that 12 months from then Chernyakhovsky, Rokossovsky, Zhukov, and Konev had far more freedom of action. But by then, from Tilsit to the Polish Carpathians, the German Army was little more than a ruin.

What is certain is that Stalin showed himself eminently satisfied by the way in which Zhukov and those under him had conducted the business; the proof of it being that on February 23, 1944 a decree of the Praesidium of the Supreme Council of the U.S.S.R. conferred upon General of the Army Konev the title of Marshal of the Soviet Union and upon General Rotmistrov that of Marshal of Tank Forces.

▽ The Korsun' pocket as seen by the Soviet artist Krivonogov.

CHAPTER 107
Exit Manstein

No sooner had the Russians closed the ring around XI and XLII Corps, than Field-Marshal von Manstein, just installed in the H.Q. which he had had transferred from Vinnitsa to Proskurov, learnt that the 3rd and 4th Ukrainian Fronts' forces had begun a combined attack on the Nikopol' bridgehead. But he was soon spared the anxiety of having to wage two defensive battles simultaneously, for on February 2, by order of O.K.H., the 6th Army, which was fighting in this sector, was transferred from Army Group "South" to Army Group "A".

It was, in fact, a rather poor legacy that Manstein bequeathed to Field-Marshal von Kleist, since the four corps comprising the 6th Army were completely worn out and, in addition, were firmly held in a pincer movement between the 3rd and 4th Ukrainian Fronts' forces; though the thick mud would soon thwart Generals Malinovsky and Tolbukhin in their attempt to benefit strategically from the tactical advantages which their superior resources had given them.

On February 3, General Malinovsky's 46th and 8th Armies reached Apostolovo, 30 miles from Nikopol', at the same time as the 4th Ukrainian Front's forces were going in to storm this latter town's defences on the left bank of the Dniepr. Whereupon a command from the Führer ordered General von Vormann to send in his 24th Panzer Division; but this formation, though most ably commanded by Lieutenant-General M. von Edelsheim, arrived too late to plug the gap in the line at Apostolovo, as Wöhler and Manstein had tried to tell Hitler it would.

Against the Nikopol' bridgehead General Tolbukhin sent in no fewer than 12 infantry and two armoured divisions; General F. Schörner defended it with six infantry divisions and the two Panzer divisions of his XXX Corps. However, the strength of the former had been reduced to that of just one regiment, whilst on the day of the attack, the Panzer divisions had only five sound tanks. Despite the strong Nazi convictions which imbued Schörner and made him resist with great courage, he was pushed back from the right bank of the Dniepr, leaving behind him large quantities of *matériel;* on February 9, the 4th Ukrainian Front's forces liberated Nikopol', though the important engineering centre of Krivoy-Rog was not taken by the 3rd Ukrainian Front forces until February 22. By the end of the month the German 6th Army, in considerable disarray, had taken up positions behind the Ingulets, a tributary of the Dniepr, which flows into it just east of Kherson.

▽ and ▷ Once again the spring rasputitsa *engulfed the Eastern Front battlefields in mud and slush. In the spring of 1943 it had caused Manstein's great counter-offensive to peter out; now, in 1944, the slowing-down of the war of movement favoured the hard-pressed Wehrmacht.*
▷ ▽ Victims of the winter fighting are brought to light by the thaw.

The Russians roll on

Whilst the 6th Army's retreat considerably shortened the line that Kleist now had to hold, Manstein's stretched between Vinnitsa and Rovno; furthermore, there had been heavy losses in the fighting at Korsun', Nikopol', and Krivoy-Rog, with the Panzer divisions in particular being reduced to an average of about 30 tanks, about 20 per cent of their normal strength

of 152 Pzkw IV and V tanks.

According to the calculations of Army Group "South", January and February had been expensive months for the enemy, who had lost 25,353 prisoners, 3,928 tanks, and 3,536 guns; but as Manstein rightly points out in his memoirs:

"These figures only served to show the enormous resources at the Red Army's command. The Russians were no longer merely hurling in infantrymen–the drop in the number of prisoners to the amount of arms captured or destroyed showed either that they had been able to save men by sacrificing arms and equipment, or that they had suffered enormous losses in manpower."

At Rastenburg, the Germans were counting upon the combined effects of these losses and of the thaw to slow down, then halt, the Russian advance. The staff sections of Army Group "South" were much less optimistic: the Russians still had 50 to 100 tanks per tank corps, making a total of 1,500 against less than 400 for the Germans. Secondly, radio Intelligence showed that between Rovno and Mozyr' another front, the 1st Belorussian Front (commanded by General Rokossovsky) was coming into being.

Faced with this information, Manstein reformed as best he could to reinforce his 4th *Panzerarmee,* which barred the enemy's advance towards Ternopol' and Chernovtsy. Thus Generals Wöhler and Hube were forced to give up five Panzer divisions to Raus, who also received three infantry divisions from O.K.H.

Vatutin's death

Despite these reinforcements, the 4th Army was destroyed on the very first day–March 4–of the new offensive launched by the 1st Belorussian Front's armies, now commanded by Marshal Zhukov. What, then, had happened to his predecessor, General Vatutin? The only thing one can state for sure is that he died at Kiev on April 14, 1944. But how? At the time of his death, a Moscow communiqué stated that it was from the after effects of a chill caught at the front. But the Soviet academician Telpukhovsky affirms "that this ardent defender of his socialist mother-country, this eminent general and Soviet army commander"–a judgement with which none will disagree–died as the result of bullet wounds inflicted by the enemy. In November 1961, however, during the twenty-second Congress of the Russian Communist Party, Nikita Khruschev, who had been Vatutin's political aide, revealed to an astonished audience that the liberator of Kiev had committed suicide whilst suffering from a fit of nervous depression. This is the version related by Michel Garder in his book *A War Unlike The Others,* published in 1962. It should be noted, however, that he does not accept this story himself, and in fact declares it to be highly unlikely. Finally, Alexander Werth, who during the war was the *Sunday Times'* Russian correspondent, brought out yet another explanation. According to him, Vatutin had been ambushed and killed by a band of Ukrainian nationalists: a version which has the advantage of explaining why Khruschev, himself a Ukrainian, might have distorted the facts.

The offensive restarts

At all events, Zhukov, on going into battle on March 4, 1944, had under him three tank and six rifle armies, i.e. about 60 divisions and at least 1,000 tanks. Attacking on both sides of Shepetovka on a front of about 120 miles, he gained between 15 and 30 miles in less than 48 hours, so that by March 6 his 3rd Guards Tank Army was approaching the L'vov–Odessa railway line at Volochisk, the last but one communication and supply link for Army Group "South" before the Carpathians.

By March 9, having covered some 80 miles in less than six days, General Rybalko's tanks came up against the hastily improvised Ternopol' defences. At the same time, the 1st *Panzerarmee* and the German 8th Army were being severely mauled by the left wing of Zhukov's forces and the 2nd Ukrainian Front, numbering seven rifle and two tank armies. Immediately the forces of Generals Hube and Wöhler, which had not yet recovered from their losses at Korsun', and had had part of their Panzer units transferred to Raus, buckled under the shock. In particular, the 8th Army was forced to withdraw towards Uman'.

Manstein, however, was not surprised by this new Russian offensive, whose purpose he saw only too clearly. *Stavka*'s aim was, in fact, nothing less than the cutting off of Army Groups "South" and "A" from the rest of the German troops fighting on the Eastern Front, pushing them south-west, as far as Odessa on the Black Sea, where they would stand no more chance of being evacuated than the defenders of the Crimea at Sevastopol'.

◁ A carefully-posed photograph shows a German infantryman with a Panzerfaust–*an anti-tank rocket-launcher which fired a hollow-charge explosive missile.*
▽ Panzer victim: a knocked-out Pzkw IV. Notice the curved "skirt armour" around the turret, intended to explode anti-tank shells before they reached the main armour.
▽▽ Czech troops, serving with the Red Army, break cover for the attack.

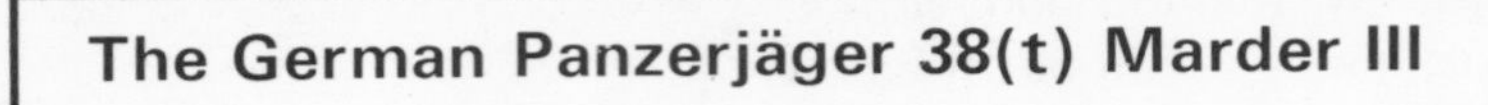

The German Panzerjäger 38(t) Marder III

Weight: 11.6 tons.
Crew: 4.
Armament: one 7.62-cm PaK 36(r) gun with 30 rounds and one 7.92-mm machine gun with 1,500 rounds. (The main armament was a rechambered Russian FK 296 or 297 anti-tank gun.)
Armour: hull front 52-mm, sides and rear 15-mm, decking 10-mm, and belly 8-mm; superstructure front and sides 16-mm; gun shield 11-mm.
Engine: one Praga EPA 6-cylinder inline, 125-hp.
Speed: 26 mph on roads, 9 mph cross-country.
Range: 115 miles on roads, 87 miles cross-country.
Length: 21 feet $1\frac{1}{4}$ inches.
Width: 7 feet 1 inch.
Height: 8 feet $2\frac{1}{2}$ inches.

Faced with such an overwhelming threat, Manstein did not hesitate. First, he ordered Generals Hube and Wöhler to withdraw immediately; then he decided to mass his troops around General Raus to stop Zhukov taking the most threatening route across the Dniestr to the Carpathians via Chernovtsy. With his XIII Corps covering L'vov in the Brody region, he ordered XLVIII Panzer Corps, then fighting 120 miles to the east, south-west of Berdichev, to go to the defence of Ternopol'. To carry out such an order, it first had to slip through the columns of the northbound 1st Ukrainian Front armies and do so without being engaged by the enemy. That it succeeded was due to the coolness and skill of its commander, General Balck, and also to errors committed by the Russians. Mellenthin, chief-of-staff of XLVIII Panzer Corps makes the following remark in this connection: "Since Russian attacks were nearly always aimed at large centres – probably because the Soviet generals wanted to attract attention to themselves by having their names inserted in special communiqués – we avoided such centres like the plague." Their manoeuvre was successful, and Manstein was able to ward off the catastrophe that had seemed so near, making the Russians fight for more than a month before they could enter Ternopol'. However, it was not his responsibility to impose his views on Kleist, and he was not going to abandon his fellow-officer, just when the latter's 6th Army was locked in battle with the 50 or 60 divisions of the 3rd and 4th Ukrainian Fronts' armies.

Hitler steps in again

At O.K.H., where the actions of the two army groups ought to have been co-ordinated, Hitler obstinately refused to allow the 6th Army to abandon the Bug line and strengthen Manstein's right wing. The consequence was that on March 13 Marshal Konev had pierced the defences that the 8th Army had hastily improvised on the right bank of the Bug, and had crossed the river on a 100-mile wide front. This breakthrough cruelly exposed the right wing of the *1st Panzerarmee,* whilst its left wing was being mercilessly hammered by Marshal Zhukov.

Ordered to Obersalzberg on March 19 to take part in a ceremony during which Rundstedt, on behalf of his fellow officers, presented vows of loyalty to the Führer, Manstein took advantage of the occasion to put his point of view: in his opinion four decisions had to be made, and quickly:
"1. Immediate withdrawal of the 6th Army behind the Dniestr. The salient it occupied on the Bug was still much too pronounced and demanded too many troops for its defence. It was Kleist himself, commanding Army Group 'A', who had proposed this;
2. The units thus freed would then be rapidly transferred to the area between the Dniestr and the Prut, preventing the 8th Army from being pushed back from the Dniestr towards the south-east;
3. Army Group 'A' to be given the clear responsibility, in liaison with Rumanian forces, for covering Rumania on the Dniestr or the Prut; and
4. A rapid strengthening of the northern wing of Army Group 'South', to prevent its being pushed back into the Carpathians, or to prevent a Russian advance on L'vov."

▽ *More mobile artillery for the Panzer arm. This is a* Hummel – *"bumble-bee" – which mounted a 15-cm gun on a Pzkw IV hull. This weapon was officially classified as* schwere Panzerhaubitze – *"heavy armoured howitzer". The 15-cm gun had been the mainstay of the German medium artillery for years.*

△ *Jetsam of defeat: German prisoners savour Russian hospitality at ration time.*

▽ *Keeping up the momentum: Russian infantry, backed by armour.*

But Hitler remained intractable; there were to be neither substantial reinforcements, nor freedom of manoeuvre for his generals.

The Soviet Blitzkrieg

Meanwhile, in the 2nd Ukrainian Front's sector, operations were taking place at Blitzkrieg speed, and even so farseeing a commander as Manstein was being left behind by events. Almost at the same time as he was suggesting to Hitler that the 6th and 8th Armies be withdrawn behind the Dniestr, Marshal Rotmistrov's 5th Guards Tank Army and General Kravchenko's 6th Army reached and crossed the river on either side of the town of Soroki.

Worse still, on March 21, Marshal Zhukov, who had regrouped his forces after his moderate success at Ternopol', attacked the point just where the commands of General Raus and Hube came together. Throwing three tank armies into the attack, he broke through and immediately advanced south; by the 23rd his forward troops had reached the Dniestr at Chernovtsy, with the resultant danger that the 1st *Panzerarmee,* fightin near Proskurov on the Bug, would be cu off. It had to be ordered to move west an try to make contact with the 4th Army, fc already the only means of supplying was by airlift.

After a whole day spent in sending an receiving a series of curt telephone call Manstein was peremptorily summone to the Berghof. Here he was received b Hitler at about noon on March 25, and was only after hours of discussion, an Manstein's threat to resign his com mand, that Hitler gave in on the two point he was most insistent upon: firstly, h was authorised to tell Hube to fight hi way through to the west, and secondly h was assured that he would very soon b reinforced by the *Waffen*-S.S. II Panze Corps which, in case there was a cros Channel landing, was stationed nea Alençon.

But this meeting had lost the German 48 hours, of which the Russians took ful advantage: on March 27, the Russia 1st and 4th Tank Armies, commande respectively by Generals D. D Lelyushenko and K. S. Moskalenkc joined up at Sekiryany, on the Dniestr' right bank, and behind the 1st *Panzerar mee.* Hube was thus caught in a trap nea

The Russian T-34/85 medium tank

Weight: 32 tons.
Crew: 5.
Armament: one M1944 85-mm gun with 56 rounds and two 7.62-mm Degtyarev machine guns with 2,745 rounds.
Armour: hull glacis, nose, sides, and rear 47-mm, decking 30-mm, belly 20-mm; turret front 90-mm, sides 75-mm, rear 60-mm, and roof 20-mm.
Engine: one V-2-34 12-cylinder inline, 500-hp.
Speed: 32 mph on roads, 10 mph cross-country.
Range: 220 miles on roads, 125 miles cross-country.
Length: 24 feet 9 inches.
Width: 9 feet 10 inches.
Height: 7 feet 11 inches.

△△ *Aftermath of battle in a Ukrainian village street. Russian soldiers examine the bodies.*
△ *A pause during the long retreat for a* Waffen-S.S. *motorised unit.*

Skala-Podolskaya with about ten divisions, including three Panzer divisions, and there is no doubt that disaster would have struck south of the Pripet, if this brave general, who had lost an arm in World War I, had not shown such optimism, resolution, and skill, and inspired such confidence in his troops, both officers and other ranks.

Manstein finally sacked by Hitler

Did Hitler regret having agreed to Manstein's suggestions, or did he think him less capable than General Model of lessening the damage that his own stubbornness had caused in the first place? Whatever the reason, on March 30, Manstein, the victor of Sevastopol' and Khar'kov, took the plane to Obersalzberg, where at one and the same time, he was awarded the Oak Leaves to the Knight's Cross of the Iron Cross and relieved of the command which he had assumed in such grim circumstances on November 24, 1942.

"For a long time Göring and Himmler had been conspiring towards my downfall," wrote Manstein. "I knew this. But the main reason was that on March 25 Hitler had been obliged to grant me what he had previously, and in public, refused me. On shaking hands to take leave of him, I said 'I hope your decision today will not turn out to be mistaken.'

"Kleist was received after me and

dismissed in like fashion. As we left the Berghof, we saw our successors, Colonel-General Model, who was going to take over my army group which would now be called Army Group 'North Ukraine' and General Schörner, Kleist's replacement, already waiting at the door!"

And so, on April 2, Colonel-General Walther Model, in whom Hitler recognised the best repairer of his own mistakes, took command of what a few days later was rather pompously re-christened Army Group "North Ukraine".

Major-General Mellenthin who, as chief-of-staff of XLVIII Panzer Corps, got to know Model well, describes him as a "small thin man, jovial and lively, whom one could never have imagined separated from his monocle. But, however great his single-mindedness, his energy or his courage, he was very different from Manstein. In particular, Model was only too prone to busy himself with every tiniest detail, and to tell his army commanders, and even his corps commanders, where and how they were to draw up their troops. General Balck, for example, the commander of XLVIII Panzer Corps, considered this tendency in his new chief to be most irritating."

Hube wins through

At the same time as Hube's "mobile pocket" was painfully fighting its way west, Zhukov had crossed the Dniestr and reached the foothills of the Carpathians, first having captured Chernovtsy, Kolomyya, and Nadvornaya. It was at this time that the II S.S. Panzer Corps, comprising the 9th and 10th *"Hohenstaufen"* and *"Frundsberg"* Panzer Divisions, arrived in the L'vov region, under the command of Colonel-General P. Hausser. In addition Hitler had made available to Army Group "South" the 367th Division and the 100th *Jäger* Division, which had just taken part in the invasion of Hungary. Thanks to these reinforcements, Generals Model and Raus succeeded on April 9 in re-establishing contact at Buchach on the River Strypa (one of the Dniestr's left bank tributaries) with the 1st *Panzerarmee* which, despite a retreat of some 120 miles through enemy territory, and having to cross four rivers, had managed to save most of its equipment. A few days later Hube was killed in an air accident *en route* to receive promotion from Hitler.

▽ Weary and dispirited German infantry reveal the strain of the fighting for the Dniepr bend. Only the man on the left has managed to crack a smile for the camera.

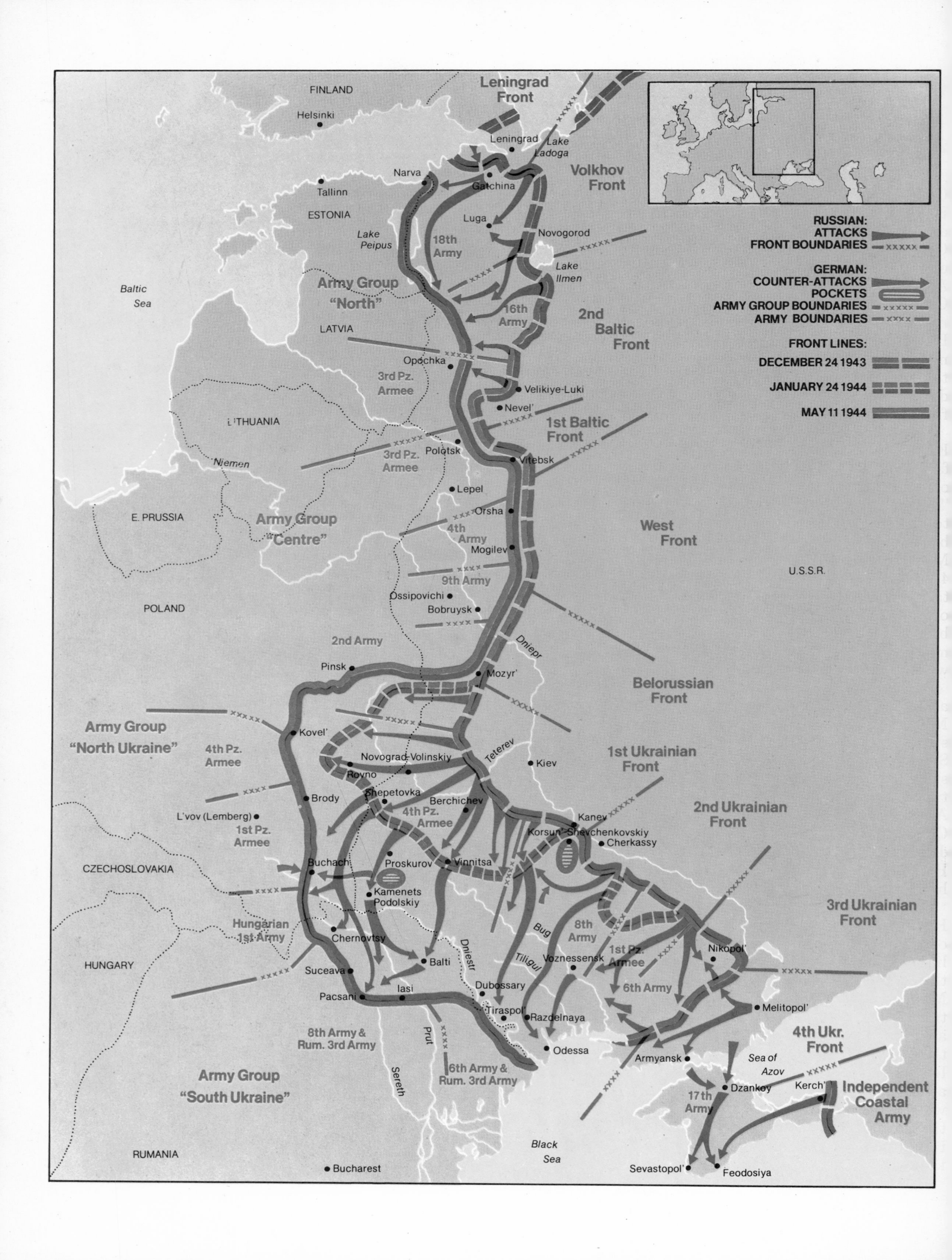

RUSSIAN:
ATTACKS
FRONT BOUNDARIES
GERMAN:
COUNTER-ATTACKS
POCKETS
ARMY GROUP BOUNDARIES
ARMY BOUNDARIES
FRONT LINES:
DECEMBER 24 1943
JANUARY 24 1944
MAY 11 1944
FINLAND
Helsinki
Leningrad Front
Leningrad
Lake Ladoga
Volkhov Front
Narva
Gatchina
Tallinn
ESTONIA
Luga
Novogorod
Lake Peipus
18th Army
Lake Ilmen
Baltic Sea
Army Group "North"
16th Army
2nd Baltic Front
LATVIA
Opochka
3rd Pz. Armee
Velikiye-Luki
Nevel'
LITHUANIA
1st Baltic Front
Polotsk
Vitebsk
Niemen
Lepel
Orsha
E. PRUSSIA
Army Group "Centre"
4th Army
West Front
Mogilev
9th Army
U.S.S.R.
Ossipovichi
Bobruysk
POLAND
2nd Army
Dniepr
Pinsk
Mozyr'
Belorussian Front
Army Group "North Ukraine"
Kovel'
4th Pz. Armee
Teterev
1st Ukrainian Front
Novograd-Volinskiy
Kiev
Rovno
Brody
Shepetovka
Berchichev
2nd Ukrainian Front
L'vov (Lemberg)
1st Pz. Armee
Kanev
Korsun'-Shevchenkovskiy
Cherkassy
Buchach
Proskurov
Vinnitsa
CZECHOSLOVAKIA
Kamenets Podolskiy
3rd Ukrainian Front
Hungarian 1st Army
Bug
8th Army
Chernovtsy
Dniestr
Nikopol'
Tiligul
HUNGARY
Balti
Voznessensk
Suceava
Iasi
Dubossary
6th Army
Pacsani
Tiraspol'
Razdelnaya
Melitopol'
8th Army & Rum. 3rd Army
Prut
Odessa
4th Ukr. Front
Armyansk
Sea of Azov
Sereth
6th Army & Rum. 3rd Army
Army Group "South Ukraine"
Dzankoy
Kerch'
Independent Coastal Army
17th Army
Black Sea
RUMANIA
Bucharest
Sevastopol'
Feodosiya

CHAPTER 108

Back to the Crimea

)n March 30, like his colleague Manstein, Kleist had at the same time been decorated and dismissed; fortunately his successor, General Schörner, was a man after his own heart. A few days earlier, the 8th Army had been transferred to Army Group "A", which a week later was renamed Army Group "South Ukraine". But by the end of the month Schörner no longer held a square inch of Ukrainian territory–in fact, he considered he had done well to save the 6th and 8th Armies from complete disaster.

The Dniestr having been forced by Konev's armour, the 8th Army was soon face to face with the prospect of being cut off from all contact with Army Group "South", and of being pushed right back to the mouth of the Danube. Thanks, however, to the rapidity with which Marshal Antonescu moved his Rumanian 4th Army into the line, and to the splendid tactical sense of General Wöhler, not only was this disaster avoided, but also a break between Model and Schörner, who maintained contact at Kuty, 40 miles west of Chernovtsy.

This success, however, was obtained at the cost of northern Bessarabia and Moldavia, for the Prut was no more successful than the Dniestr in halting the Soviet tank advance. In fact, all that the stiffening of Germano–Rumanian resistance managed to accomplish, in mid-April, was to stop the Russians in front of Chişinau in Bessarabia and Iasi in Moldavia, though the towns of Botoşani, Paşcani, and Suceava fell into their hands.

The German 6th Army, which by Hitler's express command had been kept on the lower Bug beyond all reasonable limits, almost suffered the same fate in the Odessa region as at Stalingrad. Malinovsky and the 3rd Ukrainian Front tried to turn a good situation to their advantage by pushing through the gap that had been made between the 6th Army's left flank and the right of the 8th Army as a result of the Uman' breakthrough, with the obvious aim of cutting it off from the Dniestr; and it has to be admitted that it had plenty of resources to accomplish this.

However, Hitler, judging by the directive he issued on April 2 to the commanders of Army Groups "A", "South", and "Centre", did not seem to think the situation so dangerous, since he ordered Schörner to hold "for the time being, the line of the Tiligul estuary to Dubossary on the Dniestr until such time as it would be possible to supply the Crimea independently of Odessa. The retreat to the Dniestr ought, however, still to be prepared."

The position to be occupied by the 6th

▽ *Russian poster: the bayonet of the Red Army tears into the Nazi wolf.*

Army between the estuary of the Tiligul and Dubossary on the Dniestr's left bank, level with the city of Chişinau, was about 120 miles long. With the completely worn-out troops that General Hollidt had, such a line could not be held indefinitely, even if he had been allowed sufficient time to dig himself in and organise himself.

The enterprising Malinovsky took good care, however, to allow him no time; on April 5, supported by the guns of a whole corps of artillery, he captured the Tiligul position, whilst the squadrons and tanks of the Kuban' Cavalry Corps, commanded by Lieutenant-General Pliev, took the railway junction of Razdelnaya by surprise, thus cutting off the enemy's access to the Dniestr crossings at Tiraspol. Faced with these reverses, which placed him in a catastrophic position, the 6th Army's commander took it upon himself, on April 9, to evacuate Odessa. Crossing the Dniestr, his troops, in collaboration with the Rumanian 3rd Army, organised the defence of the river's right bank, between the Black Sea and the Dubossary region. North of Chişinau, Hollidt's left flank once more made contact with General Wöhler's right. In Stalin's special communiqué, which described the liberation of Odessa in particularly glowing terms, the honour of this victory went to the gallant defenders of Stalingrad: Colonel-General Chuikov and his 62nd Army.

Crisis in the Crimea

The April 2 directive, from which we have just quoted, showed Hitler's resolution to defend the Crimea at all costs. Less than a week later, the storm clouds which Kleist and Manstein had seen gathering burst with irresistible force. Within Army Group "A", it was the German 17th Army under the command of Colonel-General C. Jaenecke, and comprising V and IL Corps and the Rumanian I Mountain Corps, themselves made up of five German divisions and seven Rumanian divisions, which had the task of defending the peninsula. It must, however, be said that two of the Rumanian divisions were in action against the partisans who, since November 1943, had held the Krimskiye massif, whose peaks dominate the southern coast of the Crimea. The key to the Crimea

▽ *The inevitable* rasputitsa *of spring. Here German troops are attempting to extricate a half-track stuck in the mud somewhere near Lake Ilmen.*

the Kamenskoye isthmus, was held by IL Corps (General R. Konrad), who had established his 50th, 111th, and 336th Divisions in soundly fortified positions defending this tongue of land, whilst the Rumanian 9th Cavalry Division kept watch on the Black Sea, and the Rumanian 10th and 19th Divisions performed the same task on the coast of the Sivash Sea. V Corps (General K. Allmendinger) kept an eye on the small bridgehead which the Russians had taken the previous autumn beyond the Kerch' Strait, a task in which it was helped by the 73rd and 98th Divisions, and the 6th Cavalry Division and 3rd Mountain Division of the Rumanian Army.

Stavka's plan

Stavka's plan to reconquer the peninsula meant the simultaneous action of the 4th Ukrainian Front and a separate army, known as the Independent Coastal Army. The first, with 18 infantry divisions and four armoured corps, would storm the Kamenskoye isthmus, whilst the second, 12 divisions strong, would break out of the Kerch' bridgehead, and they would then together converge upon Sevastopol'. As will be noted, the Russians had ensured a massive superiority in men and *matériel*.

On April 8, General Tolbukhin unleashed the offensive, the 4th Ukrainian Front attacking under an air umbrella as large as it was powerful.

On the right, the 2nd Guards Army, under Lieutenant-General G. F. Zakharov, was hard put to it to storm the Kamenskoye defences, and took 48 hours to reach the outskirts of Armyansk. On the left, breaking out of the small bridgehead on the Sivash Sea, which it had succeeded in linking to the mainland by means of a dike, the 51st Army, commanded by Lieutenant-General Ya. G. Kreizer, which had the main task, had in fact a much easier job, faced as it was by only the two Rumanian divisions. By midday on April 9, the 10th Division was submerged, and its collapse enabled the Soviet tanks to capture two days later the important junction of Dzhanskoy, where the railway leading to Sevastopol' divides from that leading to the town of Feodosiya and the port of Kerch'.

On April 11, in the Kerch' peninsula, the Independent Coastal Army, under General Eremenko, attacked in its turn; and when one realises that Hitler, a prey to hesitation, thought he could conduct the Crimea campaign from Obersalzberg, it was little short of a miracle that General Jaenecke was able to withdraw his troops to their Sevastopol' positions without being intercepted by the combined forces of Tolbukhin and Eremenko, who had linked up on April 16 near Yalta. To defend its 25-mile long front before Sevastopol', the 17th Army could now count only upon the five German divisions already mentioned above. But they had been reduced, on average, to something like a third of their normal strength and were already tired. Therefore Schörner flew to see the Führer personally and put the case for the evacuation of his troops. In vain, however, and when Jaenecke, in his turn, went to Berchtesgaden to put the same arguments, he was even refused permission to return to Sevastopol', and was succeeded as head of the 17th Army, on April 27, by General Allmendinger.

On May 7, after artillery had softened up the positions for 48 hours, the 2nd Guards Army attacked the northern flank, as Manstein had done in 1942; but the Germans were too few to rival the

▽ *German rolling stock destroyed by the Russians' tactical air forces. These, combined with the increasing success of partisans behind the German lines, made supply a constant problem for the army.*

∆ *Covered by a smoke screen, a Russian munitions barge crosses the Kerch' strait towards the Crimea. Here Hitler's grandiose idea of renewing the German push through the Caucasus would meet its end.*

heroic exploits of General Petrov's men. Thus, when General Allmendinger finally received a message on May 9 from the Führer authorising evacuation, it was already too late for it to be properly organised, especially since the Soviet Air Force, completely dominating the air, fired at anything that tried to take to the sea. On May 13, all resistance ceased in the region around the Khersonesskiy (Chersonese) peninsula, now (as in 1942) the last defence position.

The evacuation of the Crimea gave rise to dramatic scenes such as those described by Alexander Werth:

"For three days and nights, the Chersonese was that 'unspeakable inferno' to which German authors now refer. True, on the night of May 9–10 and on the following night, two small ships did come and perhaps 1,000 men were taken aboard. This greatly encouraged the remaining troops." But the Russians had no intention of letting the Germans get away by sea:

"And on the night of May 11–12 the *katyusha* mortars ('the Black Death' the Germans used to call them) came into action. What followed was a massacre. The Germans fled in panic beyond the second and then the third line of their defences, and when, in the early morning hours, Russian tanks drove in, they began to surrender in large numbers, among them their commander, General Böhme, and several other staff officers who had been sheltering in the cellar of the only farm building on the promontory.

"Thousands of wounded had been taken to the tip of the promontory, and here were also some 750 SS-men who refused to surrender, and went on firing. A few dozen survivors tried in the end to get away by sea in small boats or rafts. Some of these got away, but often only to be machine-gunned by Russian aircraft. These desperate men were hoping to get to Rumania, Turkey, or maybe to be picked up by some German or Rumanian vessel."

The 17th Army's losses were very heavy. On April 8 it had comprised 128,500 German and 66,000 Rumanian troops; of these, 96,800 Germans and 40,200 Ru-

∇ *Part of the Russian haul: stacks of rifles and helmets abandoned by the Germans at Khersonesskiy.*

manians were evacuated, leaving behind 31,700 German and 25,800 Rumanian dead or missing. But it must be remembered that of the 137,000 evacuated, more than 39,000 were wounded and all their equipment lost.

The struggle in the north

Let us now turn from the Soviets' winter offensive south of the Pripet to the campaigns which, between January 15 and March 15, resulted in the complete relief of Leningrad through the rout of Army Group "North".

At the beginning of the year, Field-Marshal von Küchler, with his right flank at Polotsk and his left up by the Gulf of Finland, to the west of Oranienbaum, was holding a front of more than 500 miles with 40 divisions, all infantry. This line of defence was dangerously exposed, both at Oranienbaum and south of Leningrad, as well as on the left bank of the Volkhov. Which is why, on December 30, the commander of Army Group "North" suggested to Hitler that he withdraw his 16th and 18th Armies to the "Panther" position which was then being prepared; this would reduce the front by more than 60 miles; and of the remaining 440 miles,

△ *German prisoners in the ruins of Sevastopol'. Extraordinarily, the Germans failed to offer the type of last-ditch defence that had so characterised the Russian effort in 1942.*
◁ *May 8, 1944: Soviet sailors enter Sevastopol'.*
Overleaf: *German* Panzergrenadiers *pull back through a burning village near Kiev.*

△ *A Panther tank meets its end.*
△▷ *A Russian anti-tank gun and its crew lie in wait for prey.*
▷▷ *German* Panzergrenadiers *aboard their battlefield transport.*

more than 120 miles consisted of Lake Peipus and 50 of the expanse of water formed by the junction of the Gulf of Finland with the mouth of the Narva.

Although such a withdrawal would have saved eight divisions, Hitler rejected Küchler's suggestion, for he was fully aware that the Russian and Finnish Governments had resumed diplomatic contact at Stockholm; thus to abandon the positions held by Army Group "North" might encourage Finland to bow out of the war.

The 18th Army caught

In the meantime, on January 14 the Leningrad Front's armies, under General Govorov, attacked the left wing of the German 18th Army, commanded by Colonel-General von Lindemann. According to German authorities, Govorov commanded a force of 42 infantry divisions and nine tank corps, though these figures cannot be checked since Soviet historians such as Telpukhovsky give no information on the strength of the Red Army forces on this occasion. Simultaneously, General Meretskov's Volkhov Front forces, with 18 infantry and 15 tank divisions, attacked the right wing of the 18th Army in the Novgorod sector.

Thus this offensive planned by *Stavka* took the form of a pincer movement, with Govorov and Meretskov trying to meet at Luga, so catching Lindemann's 18 divisions in the trap.

On the Leningrad Front, the Soviet aim was to reduce the Peterhof salient, and to this end, General Fedyuninsky's 2nd Shock Army, from the Oranienbaum bridgehead, and General Maslennikov's 42nd Army were to aim for the common objective of Gatchina. The Germans, behind well-established defensive positions, put up a very stubborn resistance, and held out for nearly a week. But once the 126th, 170th, and 215th Divisions collapsed, a large gap was opened up in the German positions. On January 26, Govorov reached Pushkin, formerly Tsarskoye-Selo, and extended his offensive right up to the Mga region, a victory which enabled the Russians to capture large quantities of arms, in particular 85 guns of greater than 10-inch calibre.

On the Volkhov front, General Meretskov's capture of Lyuban' enabled direct

railway communication between Moscow and Leningrad to be re-established; whilst north of Lake Ilmen, his left flank, comprising the 59th Army, commanded by General Korovnikov, punched a gaping hole in the German defences, recaptured Novgorod, and speeded up its advance towards the west. On January 21 the plan prepared by Marshal Zhukov entered the phase of exploitation.

Küchler sacked

With both wings of his army in disarray, and no reinforcements except the single 12th Panzer Division, Küchler realised the necessity of withdrawing the 18th Army to the Luga as a matter of urgency, only to see himself immediately relieved of his command in favour of Colonel-General Model. Monstrously unjust as this decision was, it nevertheless helped to save Army Group "North", since Hitler showed himself more ready to listen to a commander of working-class origin than to the aristocratic Küchler; and the day after his appointment, Model was given two more divisions.

▲ *Field-Marshal Erich von Manstein. Sacked in April 1944, his dismissal was permanent, unlike that of several other senior commanders. Liddell Hart described him as "the Allies' most formidable military opponent–a man who combined modern ideas of manoeuvre, a mastery of technical detail and great driving power".*
▶ *An exhausted German soldier rests on the trail of a destroyed gun.*

Field-Marshal Walther Model was born in 1891. He was chief-of-staff of IV Corps in the Polish campaign and of 16th Army in the French. He commanded the 3rd Panzer Division in "Barbarossa" and 9th Army in 1942. Always in favour with Hitler, Model was instrumental in getting *"Zitadelle"* postponed until July 1943, when he failed to stem the Russian counter-offensive at Orel. In 1944 he was successively head of Army Groups "North", "South", and "Centre". Model was then transferred to the West as supreme commander and then head of Army Group "B".

On the whole, Model, a capable soldier, adopted the arrangements made by his predecessor, and moreover managed to get them approved by Hitler. However, hardly had he got his army from out of the clutches of Govorov, than the latter, enlarging the radius of his activities, crossed the River Luga to the left of the town of the same name; Pskov, the main supply base of Army Group "North" seemed to be the objective of this push, but at the same time it seriously exposed Colonel-General Lindemann's rear. Furthermore, the left wing of General Hansen's 16th Army was beginning to wilt under the attacks of General Popov and his Baltic Front, and to make matters worse, was in great danger of being flooded by the waters of Lake Ilmen.

This last extension of the Soviet offensive forced Model to abandon his intention of placing his 18th Army as a defensive barrier between Lake Ilmen and Lake Peipus. He asked for, and obtained, permission from O.K.H. to withdraw all his forces back to the "Panther" line, which, stretching from a point west of Nevel', passed through Opochka and Pskov, then followed the western bank of Lake Peipus, finally reaching the Gulf of Finland at Narva. Begun on February 17, this withdrawal was concluded by mid-March without any untoward incident. When Model was called upon to replace Manstein a fortnight later, Lindemann succeeded him at the head of Army Group "North", being in turn succeeded at the head of the 18th Army by General Loch.

For the German Army, therefore, the first quarter of 1944 was marked by a long series of reverses, which, although their worst effects had been avoided, had nevertheless been very costly in terms of men and materials. And many reports originating at the front showed that reinforcements were arriving without the necessary training.

The threat to Rumania

Furthermore, the protective glacis of *"Festung Europa"* was being seriously encroached upon. Bucharest and the vital oil wells of Ploiești, Budapest and the Danube basin, Galicia with its no less vital wells at Borislaw, Riga and the central Baltic, were all coming within the compass of Soviet strategy. So that these further defeats of the Third Reich had far more than merely military significance, and encroached upon the diplomatic and political plane.

As we have seen, Hitler was afraid that the withdrawal of Army Group "North" to its "Panther" defensive position might tempt Finland, which he knew to be engaged in discussions with Russia, to get out of the war and conclude a separate peace. Küchler's defeat and the battered state in which the 16th and 18th Armies reached the "Panther" line encouraged the Finns to continue their negotiations. These were broken off, however, on April 1, when the Russians insisted that all German troops should be evacuated or interned within 30 days, and that the Finns should pay them 600 million dollars in reparations, to be paid in five annual instalments.

A few days earlier, however, on March 27, whilst Hitler was talking to Admiral Horthy at Klessheim about the new "arrangements" that would have to be made in view of the line taken by the Kallay cabinet, 11 German divisions, carrying out Operation *"Margarethe"*, proceeded to occupy Hungary.

"What was I to do?" asks the former Regent in his memoirs. "It was quite clear that my abdication would not prevent the occupation of Hungary, and would allow Hitler to install a government entirely composed of Nazis, as the example of Italy clearly showed. 'Whilst I am still Regent,' I told myself, 'the Germans will at least have to show some consideration. They will be forced to keep me at the head of the army, which they will not be able to absorb into the German Army. Nor will they be able to place at the head of the government Hungarian Nazi puppets, who would hunt down, not only many Hungarian patriots, but also 800,000 Jews, and tens of thousands of refugees who had found shelter in our country. I could very conveniently have abdicated at that time and saved myself many criticisms. But I could not leave a sinking ship which at that moment had the greatest possible need of its captain.'"

In line with this reasoning, Horthy accepted the *fait accompli,* and on March 23 swore in a new cabinet, whose prime minister was General Dome-Sztojay, his ambassador in Berlin. But Hitler's Klessheim trap freed him from any obligation *vis-à-vis* the Third Reich, and henceforth the old Admiral was to embark upon a policy of resistance.

CHAPTER 109

ANZIO: failure or foundation?

A map on the scale of 1:1,000,000 is sufficient to give us an immediate picture of the results of the Soviet winter offensive in the first quarter of 1944, but to follow the Allies' progress in Italy the scale would have to be at least 1:100,000. Even on this scale we would not find all the heights and place names we shall be mentioning in our narrative.

A cartoonist in the Third Reich showed a map of Italy at this time as a boot, up which a snail, wearing the Allied flags, is slowly climbing. At about Easter, Allied public opinion did not attempt to conceal its disappointment, not to say impatience, at the results of Anglo-American strategy in the Mediterranean. As can well be imagined, political and military leaders in London and Washington were hardly able to pacify these frustrations by making public the vast organisation, training, and preparation then going on towards an operation which was to bear its first fruits at dawn on June 6. Certainly after five months of marking time the Allies scored complete victory over their enemy in Italy, but only less than 30 days before the Normandy landings and thus a little late in the day. The normal course of development of Allied strategy was hindered by a chain of unfortunate circumstances which, it must be said, had nothing to do with politics.

On January 16, 1944 the American 5th Army, still under the command of Lieutenant-General Mark Clark, renewed its attack on the Cassino redoubt, which was defended by XIV Panzer Corps from the 10th Army (General von Vietinghoff-Scheel). The main objective of this under-

▽ *American soldiers splash ashore at Anzio on January 22. The Allies gained complete strategic surprise by the landing, which went in against negligible opposition. It took the Germans some six hours to realise that an invasion was in progress behind the Cassino front.*
◁ *D.U.K.W. amphibious trucks head out to the transports to take on more loads.*

US140

taking in such difficult terrain was to force Kesselring to move up the reinforcements at present around Rome to strengthen his front. When this had been achieved, the American VI Corps (Major-General John P. Lucas), which was to effect a surprise landing on the beaches at Anzio and Nettuno, would find the way open to drive inland and attack the enemy's communications. This was the fundamental idea of Operation "Shingle", a pet scheme of Churchill, who had succeeded in winning over both Roosevelt and Stalin. He had even agreed to sacrifice to it the amphibious forces collected together for a landing on Rhodes. Did Churchill see further than his Allies? It seems likely that had the German 10th Army been annihilated during the first two weeks of February, nothing would have prevented Churchill from renewing his demands on his Allies and perhaps demanding an exploitation of this victory in the direction of Ljubljana and the abandonment of a landing in Provence, as planned at Teheran.

But everything was to go against him. First of all, General Clark considerably toned down the instructions given to him on January 12 by Sir Harold Alexander, commanding the 15th Army Group. Alexander saw the mission of the American VI Corps as follows: "to cut the enemy's main communications in the Colli Laziali (Alban Hills) area southeast of Rome, and threaten the rear of the XIV German Corps". Clark's directive of the same date to General Lucas merely required him "to seize and secure a beachhead in the vicinity of Anzio" and thence "to advance on the Colli Laziali".

This threefold manoeuvre (seize, secure, and advance) clearly did not reflect Alexander's original intention, but Alexander did not order Clark to change his directive so as to bring it into line with his own. As we shall see him giving in to his subordinate again on the following May 26, we can take it that it was not merely an oversight. We must believe that in acting as he did, General Clark was still under the strain of the Salerno landings, though he says nothing of this in his memoirs. John Lucas, entrusted with carrying out Operation "Shingle", noted in his diary: "It will be worse than the Dardanelles". His friend George S. Patton, spitting fire and smelling a fight in the offing, had said to him:

"'John, there is no one in the Army I

Δ For the benefit of the Allies in Italy: a cynical German comment on the slow pace of the march on Rome.
◁◁ G.I.s plod through the gaping jaws of a landing ship with their equipment.
A landing ship heads inshore, packed with motor transport.

would hate to see killed as much as you, but you can't get out of this alive. Of course, you might be badly wounded. No one ever blames a *wounded* general!' He advised Lucas to read the Bible when the going got tough, and then turned to one of the VI Corps commander's aides and said, 'Look here; if things get too bad, shoot the old man in the backside; but don't you dare kill the man!'"

About a week before D-day, an ill-fated landing exercise hastily carried out in the Gulf of Salerno only served to confirm Major-General Lucas's pessimistic forecast.

The wrong analysis

The 5th Army plan to take the Cassino defile placed the main burden on the American II Corps (Major-General Geoffrey Keyes). Forcing the Rapido at San Angelo, five miles south of Cassino, it would drive up the Liri valley and its tanks would exploit the success towards Frosinone then Anzio. This action was to be supported on the right by the French Expeditionary Corps (General Juin) and on the left by the British X Corps (Lieutenant-General Sir Richard McCreery).

"It was a somewhat simple concept," wrote Marshal Juin, "revealing a bold temperament which everyone recognised in the 5th Army commander, but at the same time it was at fault in that it ignored certain strategic principles and betrayed a false notion of distances and especially of the terrain in this peninsula of Italy where mountains – and what mountains! – dominate the landscape."

Sure enough the British X Corps, though it established a bridgehead on the right bank of the Garigliano (resulting from the confluence of the Liri and the Rapido), came to grief on the slopes of Monte Maio. The American 36th Division (Major-General F. L. Walker) of II Corps was even less fortunate, losing the strip of land it had won two days before on the right bank of the Rapido with casualties of 143 dead, 663 wounded, and 875 missing. On the right the 3rd Algerian Division (General de Monsabert) and the 2nd Moroccan Division (General Dody), attacking in line abreast, captured the heights of Monna Casale and Costa San Pietro (4,920 ft). But the French Expeditionary Corps did not have the reserves to exploit this success in the direction of

Atina, from where it might have been possible to get down into the Liri valley behind the defence line along the Rapido.

General Clark had six divisions (54 battalions) and his opponent, General von Senger und Etterlin (XIV Panzer Corps), had four with only six battalions apiece. This indicates how the terrain favoured the defenders, who were also valiant, well-trained, and better led. They were, however, stretched to the limit and Vietinghoff had to ask Kesselring for reinforcements. Kesselring took it upon himself to send him the 29th and the 90th *Panzergrenadier* Divisions from Rome, where they had been held in reserve against such an eventuality.

"Considering what happened," General Westphal, at the time chief-of-staff of Army Group "C", wrote in 1953, "it was a mistake. The attack and the landing at the mouth of the Garigliano were only a diversion intended to pin down our forces and to get us to drain our resources away from Rome as far as possible. The Allied commander's aim was fully achieved." Three years later Kesselring answered this charge, though without naming Westphal, to some point:

"I was well aware of the enemy's possible moves. One of these possibilities always stood out more clearly than the others. The attack by the American II Corps and the French Expeditionary Corps on positions north of Monte Cassino was clearly linked to the fighting on the Garigliano and increased its chances of success.

"Another possibility, that is the landing, was still only a faint one. We did not know yet when or where this would be. If I had refused the request of the 10th Army's commander, his right flank could have been dented and there seemed to be no way of knowing how it could have been restored." The German field-marshal seems to have been right in his judgement

△ ◁◁ *On the quayside.*
▽ ◁◁ *Down the ramp and into Anzio town.*
▽ *Kesselring's gunners wake up: a German shell scores a near hit on D.U.K.W.s heading in towards the beaches.*
Overleaf: *Extending the limited accommodation of Anzio harbour: a floating causeway from ship to shore.*

because on the eve of the event Admiral Canaris, head of the *Abwehr,* had told him that in his opinion no Allied landing was to be expected in Italy in the near future.

The Anzio landings

No other landing in Europe or in the Pacific was as successful, and at such little cost, as that at Anzio-Nettuno in Operation "Shingle". By midnight on January 22, that is after 22 hours of operations, Rear-Admirals Frank J. Lowry of the U.S. Navy and Thomas H. Troubridge of the Royal Navy had landed 36,034 men, 3,069 vehicles, and 90 per cent of the assault equipment of the U.S. VI Corps. This comprised the British 1st Division (Major-General W. Penney), the American 3rd Division (Major-General L. K. Truscott), a regiment and a battalion of paratroops, three battalions of Rangers, and a brigade of Commandos. Losses amounted to 13 killed, 44 missing, and 97 wounded. The supporting naval forces, four light cruisers and 24 destroyers, had neutralised the fire of the shore batteries and two German battalions had been overrun on the beaches. "And that was all," wrote General Westphal as he reckoned up his weak forces. "There was nothing else in the area we could have thrown against the enemy on that same day. The road to Rome (37 miles) was now open. No-one could have prevented a force which drove on hard from entering the Eternal City. For two days after the landing we were in a breath-taking situation. Our counter-measures could only take effect after 48 hours."

Kesselring musters his strength

The General Staff of Army Group "C" had made several studies of a possible Allied landing of some strategic importance. For each hypothesis envisaged (Istria, Ravenna, Civitavecchia, Leghorn, Viareggio), the formations which would fight it had been detailed off, the routes they would have to take marked out, and their tasks laid down. Each hypothetical situation had been given a keyword. Kesselring only had to signal "*Fall*

▷ *The Anzio landings and the break-through at Cassino.*

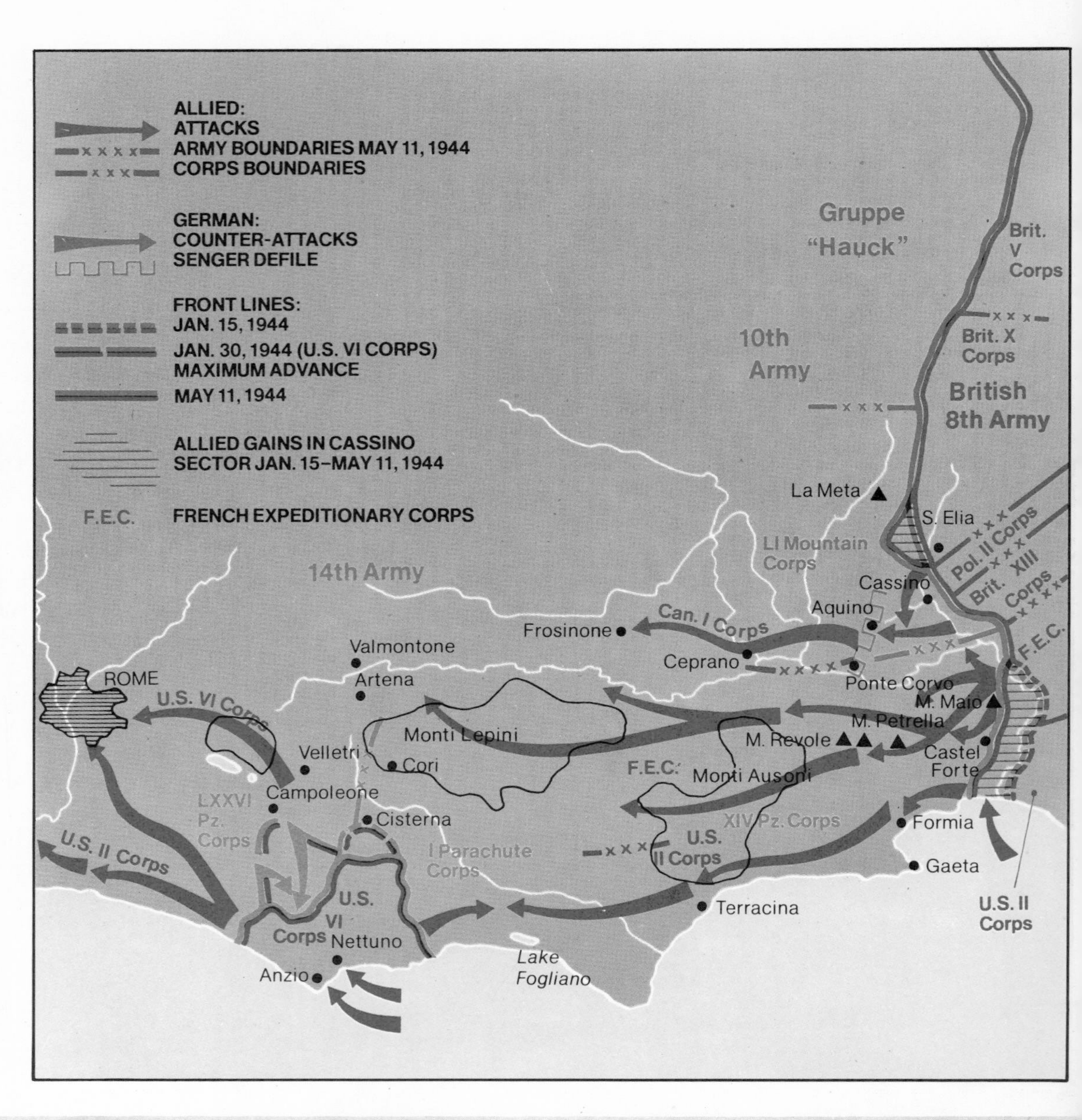

▽ *A Sherman tank heads inland from the beach-head. With the forces, both infantry and tank, available to him soon after the initial landings, could Lucas have pressed on inland and cut the Germans' communications between Rome and Cassino?*

△ *Part of 5th Army's complement (over-extravagant according to Churchill) of soft skinned and armoured vehicles.*

Richard" for the following to converge on the Anzio bridgehead:

1. the "Hermann Göring" Panzer Division from the area of Frosinone and the 4th Parachute Division from Terni, both in I Parachute Corps (General Schlemm)
2. from the Sangro front LXXVI Panzer Corps (General Herr: 26th Panzer and 3rd *Panzergrenadier* Divisions); from the Garigliano front the 29th *Panzergrenadier* Division, newly arrived in the sector; and
3. from northern Italy the staff of the 14th Army and the 65th and 362nd Divisions which had crossed the Apennines as quickly as the frost and snow would allow them.

But O.K.W. intervened and ordered Field-Marshal von Rundstedt to hand over to Kesselring the 715th Division, then stationed in the Marseilles area, and Colonel-General Löhr, commanding in the Balkans, to send him his 114th *Jäger* Division.

On January 23, when Colonel-General von Mackensen presented himself at Kesselring's H.Q. on Monte Soracte, all that lay between Anzio and Rome was a detachment of the "Hermann Göring" Panzer Division and a hotchpotch of artillery ranging from the odd 8.8-cm A.A. to Italian, French, and Yugoslav field guns. Despite the talents of Kesselring as an improviser and the capabilities of his general staff, a week was to pass before the German 14th Army could offer any consistent opposition to the Allied offensive.

On the Allied side, however, Major-General John P. Lucas thought only of consolidating his bridgehead and getting ashore the balance of his corps, the 45th Division (Major-General W. Eagles) and the 1st Armoured Division (Major-General E. N. Harmon). It will be recognised that in so doing he was only carrying out the task allotted to the 5th Army. On January 28 his 1st Armoured Division had indeed captured Aprilia, over ten miles north of Anzio, but on his right the American 3rd Division had been driven back opposite Cisterna. On the same day Mackensen had three divisions in the line and enough units to make up a fourth; by the last day of the month he was to have eight.

Was a great strategic opportunity lost between dawn on January 22 and twilight on the 28th? In London Churchill was champing with impatience and wrote to Sir Harold Alexander: "I expected to see a wild cat roaring into the mountains–and what do I find? A whale wallowing on the beaches!"

Returning to the subject in his memoirs, Churchill wrote: "The spectacle of 18,000 vehicles accumulated ashore by the fourteenth day for only 70,000 men, or less than four men to a vehicle, including drivers and attendants . . . was astonishing."

Churchill might perhaps be accused of yielding too easily to the spite he felt at the setbacks of Operation "Shingle", for which he had pleaded so eagerly to Stalin and Roosevelt. These were, however, not the feelings of the official historian of the U.S. Navy who wrote ten years after the event:

"It was the only amphibious operation in that theater where the Army was unable promptly to exploit a successful landing, or where the enemy contained Allied forces on a beachhead for a prolonged period. Indeed, in the entire war there is none to compare with it; even the Okinawa campaign in the Pacific was shorter."

We would go along with this statement, implying as it does that the blame lay here, were it not for General Truscott's opinion, which is entirely opposed to Morison's quoted above. Truscott lived through every detail of the Anzio landings as commander of the 3rd Division, then as second-in-command to General Lucas, whom he eventually replaced. He was recognised by his fellow-officers as a first-class leader, resolute, aggressive,

▽ Landing supplies in Anzio harbour.
▷ △ D.U.K.W.s on the beach at Anzio.
▷ ▽ A U.S. 155-mm "Long Tom" in action at Anzio.

and very competent. His evidence is therefore to be reckoned with:

"I suppose that armchair strategists will always labour under the delusion that there was a 'fleeting opportunity' at Anzio during which some Napoleonic figure would have charged over the Colli Laziali (Alban Hills), played havoc with the German line of communications, and galloped on into Rome. Any such concept betrays lack of comprehension of the military problem involved. It was necessary to occupy the Corps Beachhead Line to prevent the enemy from interfering with the beaches, otherwise enemy artillery and armoured detachments operating against the flanks could have cut us off from the beach and prevented the unloading of troops, supplies, and equipment. As it was, the Corps Beachhead Line was barely distant enough to prevent direct artillery fire on the beaches.

"On January 24th (i.e. on D+2) my division, with three Ranger battalions and the 504th Parachute Regiment attached, was extended on the Corps Beachhead Line, over a front of twenty miles ... Two brigade groups of the British 1st Division held a front of more than seven miles."

In his opinion again the Allied high command overestimated the psychological effect on the enemy's morale of the simple news of an Anglo-American land-

▷ *Almost like World War I all over again: a communication trench linking pillboxes in the British sector of the Anzio line.*
▽ *A British patrol pushes forward from the main Allied beach-head on a reconnaissance mission.*
▽▽ *War photographers receive their briefing in a wine cellar in Nettuno before moving to their assigned areas.*
▷▷ *British soldiers move barbed wire up towards the front in preparation for a night "wiring party". It was only in such gullies that troops on the beach-head could move around during the day without being molested by German fire.*

ing behind the 10th Army. This is shown by the text of a leaflet dropped to German troops, pointing out the apparently impossible strategic situation in which they were now caught, pinned down at Cassino and outflanked at Anzio, and urging them to surrender.

Kesselring beats Alexander to the punch

But far from allowing himself to be intimidated, Kesselring assembled his forces with a promptness underestimated by Alexander and Clark. Another reason why he was able to race them to it was because the latter were somewhat short of *matériel* for amphibious operations. The figures speak for themselves: on June 6, 1944 for a first wave of 12 divisions Eisenhower had 3,065 landing craft, whereas Anzio had 237 for four divisions.

Under these conditions, even if Lucas had had the temperament of a Patton, one could hardly have expected him to throw his forces into an attack on the Colli Laziali, over 20 miles from Anzio, with the two divisions of his first echelon and not worry also about his flanks and communications. Finally, Lucas did not have this cavalier temperament, and the day after the landings he noted in his diary: "The tension in a battle like this is terrible. Who the hell would be a general?"

Enter Hitler

The chances lost here, however, were to give rise during the months of February and March to two of the most furious battles of the war. They both ended in defeat for the attacker. On February 29 Mackensen had to abandon his attempt to crush the Anzio beach-head and Clark reported that his repeated attempts to force the Cassino defile had failed.

The battle for the beach-head arose from Hitler's initiative. On January 28 he sent Kesselring the following directive, which is worth quoting in full, so well does it reveal the Führer's state of mind on the day after the disasters suffered by Army Group "South" on the Dniepr at Kanev, and at a time when everyone was expecting an Anglo-American attack across the Channel.

"In a few days from now," he wrote "the 'Battle for Rome' will start: this will decide the defence of Central Italy and the fate of the 10th Army. But it has an even greater significance, for the Nettuno landing is the first step of the invasion of Europe planned for 1944.

"The enemy's aim is to pin down and to wear out major German forces as far as possible from the English base in which the main body of the invasion force is being held in a constant state of readiness and to gain experience for their future operations.

"The significance of the battle to be fought by the 14th Army must be made clear to each one of its soldiers.

"It will not be enough to give clear and correct tactical orders. The army, the air force, and the navy must be imbued with a fanatical determination to come

out victorious from this battle and to hang on until the last enemy soldier has been exterminated or driven back into the sea. The men will fight with a solemn hatred against an enemy who is waging a relentless war of extermination against the German people, an enemy to whom everything seems a legitimate means to this end, an enemy who, in the absence of any high ethical intention, is plotting the destruction of Germany and, along with her, that of European civilisation. The battle must be hard and without pity, and not only against the enemy but also against any leader of men who, in this decisive hour, shows any sign of weakness.

"As in Sicily, on the Rapido, and at Ortona, the enemy must be shown that the fighting strength of the German Army is still intact and that the great invasion of 1944 will be an invasion which will drown in the blood of the Anglo-Saxon soldiers."

That is why the German 14th Army, whilst it drove off the repeated attempts of the U.S. VI Corps to break out from Aprilia and to cut off the Rome–Gaeta railway at Campoleone, actively prepared to go over to the counter-attack as ordered. On February 10 a counter-attack led by the 3rd *Panzergrenadier* Division (Lieutenant-General Gräser) retook the station at Carroceto. That day the German communiqué announced 4,000 prisoners taken since January 22, whereas the Allies' figure was only 2,800. Rightly alarmed by these setbacks, General Clark sent the British 56th Division (Major-General Templer) into the bridgehead; also, at Alexander's suggestion, he appointed Truscott second-in-command of VI Corps. Meanwhile Colonel-General von Mackensen had been called to O.K.W. to put his plan for a counter-offensive before the Führer. The latter offered no objection when Mackensen explained his idea of driving his attack along the Albano–Anzio line, with diversionary attacks on either side. Hitler did not stop there, however, but took it upon himself to interfere in every detail of the plan, from which he expected wonders. Mackensen thus saw the front on which he was to attack, the troops he was to use, and even the deployment these forces were to adopt, all altered by Hitler.

The operation was entrusted to LXXVI Panzer Corps. It was to attack on a front of less than four miles with two divisions up and the 26th *Panzergrenadier* Division (Lieutenant-General von Lüttwitz) and the 20th *Panzergrenadier* Division (Lieutenant-General Fries) in army reserve. So, Hitler ordered, the infantry could be given supporting fire which would pulverise the enemy's defence. Mackensen tried in vain to point out that such a massive concentration would present a sitting target to the Anglo-American air forces and that *Luftflotte* II, under the command of Field-Marshal von Richthofen, did not have the means to fight them off. It was no good. Hitler also refused to listen to the argument that it was useless lining up the guns wheel to wheel with insufficient ammunition for them to fire at the required rate.

The attack started on February 16 as ordered by Hitler. There was a preliminary softening up by 300 guns, but the 114th and 715th Divisions, which were to advance side by side, were to be denied the support of a creeping barrage. The spongy ground of the Pontine marshes prevented the tanks and the assault guns, which were to support the waves of infantry, from getting off the roads. The 14th Army's offensive might have had the intermittent support of 20 to 30 Luftwaffe fighter-bombers, but the German troops on the ground had to withstand the assault of no less than 1,100 tons of bombs. The Anglo-American tactical air forces boxed in the battlefield and considerably hindered the movement of supplies up towards the 14th Army's front line units.

By nightfall LXXVI Panzer Corps had

◁◁ General Alexander (left) and Lieutenant-General Clark (centre), commander of the U.S. 5th Army, with Lieutenant-General McCreery (right), commander of the British X Corps. Much of the Anzio landings' ill fortune stemmed from the differing views on exploitation held by Alexander and Clark.
▽◁ German prisoners, under U.S. guard, await transport out of the Anzio area.
▽▽◁ Improvised entertainment at Anzio: "horse" racing on the throw of a dice.
▽ A wounded British soldier.
▽▽ A German "Goliath" wire-controlled tank. Ingeniously contrived to deliver an explosive charge by remote control, the "Goliath" suffered the major disadvantage of being slow and thus easily shot up.

▷ *The ruins of Anzio town.*

▽ *An American armoured car moves up towards the line through Anzio.*

advanced some three to four miles into the Allied lines and was about seven to eight miles from its objective of Anzio-Nettuno. Its guns had fired 6,500 shells, but had received ten times as many. For three days Mackensen attempted to regain the upper hand, but in vain: Truscott, who had just relieved Lucas, was too vigilant for him. On February 29, I Parachute Corps took up the attack again in the Cisterna area, but this came to a halt a few hundred yards from its point of departure. The battle around the bridgehead died down and General Clark reinforced the position with the British 5th and the American 34th Divisions. The beaches and the Allies' rear positions continued to be harassed by German heavy artillery with its observation posts up in the Colli Laziali. A hugh 11-inch railway gun in particular played havoc among the defenders. The air force was unable to silence it since, as soon as it had fired, "Leopold", as its crew, or "Anzio Annie", as the Allies called it, withdrew into a tunnel near Castel Gandolfo.

At sea, Operation "Shingle" cost Admiral Sir John Cunningham, C.-in-C. Mediterranean, the light cruisers *Spartan* and *Penelope* and three destroyers, all of the Royal Navy. Amongst the weapons used by the Germans were glide bombs and human torpedoes, the latter making their first appearance with the Kriegsmarine.

CHAPTER 110

CASSINO: breaking the stalemate

On the Cassino front General Clark strove to take up the offensive again the day after the Anzio landing. The intention was that the American II Corps, now only one division strong (the 34th, commanded by Major-General Ryder) should cross the Rapido north of Cassino whilst the French Expeditionary Corps, after taking Monte Belvedere, would move down the Liri valley, sweeping past the back of Monte Cassino. This turning movement, to be carried out as it were within rifle range, did not appeal to General Juin, who thought it would have been better to hinge the manoeuvre on Atina. Out of loyalty to General Clark, however, he did not press the point.

After rapidly regrouping at an altitude of 325 feet in the area of San Elia, the 3rd Algerian Division set off to attack its objectives: Belvedere (2,370 feet) and Colle Abate (2,930 feet).

In view of the nature of the terrain, the operation seemed to face insurmountable difficulties. Marshal Juin acknowledges this in his memoirs. Describing an occasion when he was visited by General Giraud he wrote: "The last time I had seen him was during the most critical moment of my Belvedere operation. I took him up to General Monsabert's front line H.Q., from which it was possible to watch the whole action of the Tunisian 4th *Tirailleur* Regiment. He expressed surprise that I had taken upon myself such a hazardous affair and could not refrain

△ *"My God! I'd like to have a word or two with the character who coined 'All roads lead to Rome'." Though German, this cartoon was all too apt a comment on Allied fortunes in Italy.*

▽ *General Clark awards battle streamers to a* Nisei *unit.*

from reproaching me, adding: 'I thought I was the only hot-headed fool in our army, but I see today that it's catching'."

The defile was defended by the 44th Division, a famous unit which had been re-formed after Stalingrad and which, recruited in Austria, had taken the name, famous in Prince Eugene's army, of "*Hoch und Deutschmeister*". The opposing forces were men of equal courage and tenacity. In the afternoon of January 25 the Tunisian 4th *Tirailleur* Regiment (Colonel Roux) raised the tricolour on the two heights it had scaled under withering cross-fire, but one of its battalions was virtually wiped out on the Colle Abate, whilst the other two drove off one counter-attack after another to stay on Belvedere, but only at a heavy price.

René Chambe has left this account of the dramatic combat: "Night passes. This is one of the most critical of all. From right to left the Gandoët, Bacqué, and Péponnet battalions are clinging to the sides of Hills 862, 771, and 700. The enemy is counter-attacking furiously everywhere. He is driven off by bayonet and grenade. But none of these three peaks is retaken. And ammunition runs out again; the parsimoniously distributed mouthfuls of food which make up our rations are far away. Hunger comes again and with hunger thirst, the terrible thirst which gnaws at your stomach and drills into your brain. As for sleep, that real sleep which restores, we haven't had any for a long time. Men are falling asleep now under shelling, in the midst of mines and bullets. They're killed almost before they know it. Only wounds wake them up. Some answer back, aiming their rifles and throwing their grenades in a state of half-consciousness." When it was relieved, the Tunisian 4th *Tirailleur* Regiment had lost its colonel, 39 officers, and 1,562 N.C.O.s and men: it was reduced to a third of its strength.

The Germans on their side had lost 1,200 prisoners, and to strengthen the 44th Division, which threatened at any moment to give way under the furious hammer-blows of the 3rd Algerian Division's attack, 10th Army had to send in one regiment of the 90th *Panzergrenadier* Division and another of the 71st Division, both from XIV Panzer Corps. So the French Expeditionary Corps managed to draw onto itself two-thirds of the 44 battalions then fighting opposite the American 5th Army.

The value of this force was well appreciated by General Clark. On the day after the furious fighting on Belvedere he wrote to Juin to express his admiration for the "splendid way" in which the corps had accomplished its mission, adding:

"By a carefully prepared and co-ordinated plan of operations you have launched and sustained a series of attacks which have had remarkable success in attaining their main objective, that is: to pin down by hard fighting the maximum possible number of enemy troops and thus prevent them from intervening against our landing and the establishment of our bridgehead at Anzio. By doing this you have thrown back the enemy along the whole length of your front and inflicted severe losses on troops which were already weary."

Some days later General Alexander associated himself with this praise, and these were no empty words. In his book on the Cassino battle, in which he took part the following February and March as paratroop battalion commander in the famous 1st Parachute Division, Rudolf

▽ *French gunners in action on General Juin's French Expeditionary Corps' sector of the Cassino front.*

◁ *An American mortar crew near San Vittore with white phosphorus smoke shells. The town fell to the 5th Army on January 6, 1944.*

▽ *A 17-pounder anti-tank gun manned by New Zealanders. Though German armour was scarce in Italy, anti-tank guns found useful targets in the superb emplacements that formed the backbone of Germany's Italian defence lines.*

Böhmler makes the same observation: "The greatest surprise, however, was the fighting spirit shown by the French Expeditionary Corps. The 1940 campaign had cast a sombre shadow over the French Army, and no one believed that it would ever recover from the devastating defeat that had been inflicted on it. But now General Juin's divisions were proving to be the most dangerous customers. Nor was this attributable solely to the Algerians' and Moroccans' experience in mountain warfare. Three factors combined to mould these troops into a dangerously efficient fighting force: the mountain warfare experience of the French colonial troops, the ultra-modern American equipment with which they had been equipped, and the fact that they were led by French officers who were masters of the profession of arms. With these three basic elements Juin had moulded a formidable entity. In the battles that followed, the Corps proved equal to every demand made of it, and Field-Marshal Kesselring himself assured the author that he was always uneasy about any sector of the front on which the French popped up.

"Had Clark given more heed to Juin's views in the Cassino battles and accepted his plan of thrusting via Atina into the Liri valley, the three savage battles of Cassino would probably never have been fought and the venerable House of St. Benedict would have been left unscathed."

With two divisions so hard pressed there was no question of Juin's being able to exploit his costly victory at Belvedere, which now left him in front of the rest of the Allied line. Some time afterwards he was reinforced by General Utili's motorised group, the first Italian formation to move up to the front again (having had its first taste of fighting in December). It operated on the right of the French Expeditionary Corps in the snowy massif of the Abruzzi and acquitted itself well.

In the American II Corps area, the 34th Division did not succeed in breaking out of the bridgehead it had won on the right bank of the Rapido.

The monastery destroyed

Not wishing to leave things in this state of half-failure, General Alexander put at the disposal of the 5th Army the New Zealand Corps (Lieutenant-General Freyberg), consisting of the 2nd New Zealand, the 4th Indian, and the British 78th Divisions.

But before launching his attack, General Freyberg demanded the destruction of the historic Monte Cassino abbey which

Conventional land attack having failed to make any impression on the German defences of Cassino, it was decided to let the Allied air forces have a go. The whole aerial campaign, in March, was futile. It was expensive and ultimately made the land forces' task more difficult. For the bombing razed the whole town, creating good defensive positions in the rubble for the Germans, and seriously hampering the advance of the Allies.

◁ *A low-level reconnaissance photograph taken by a U.S.A.A.F. aircraft just after the last wave of bombers had left reveals the devastation, with dust and smoke swirling above it.*

▽ ◁ *The gutted town.*

▽ *The bombing on March 15.*

Overleaf: *Aftermath of the bombing campaign.*

Above the town, at the top of Monte Cassino, stood the Abbey of St. Benedict, a religious foundation of great importance in which the body of St. Benedict was preserved. Believing quite erroneously that the Germans had turned the abbey into an observation post, the Allies bombed this too. The Germans managed to evacuate the abbot and his monks, together with the treasures, as the bombing started. And when the destruction was complete, the Germans took over the ruins.
▽ *Hits on and around the abbey.*
▽▽ *The bombardment.*
▷ *The gutted abbey.*

overlooked the Liri valley from a height of 1,700 feet. General Clark showed some scepticism when informed by his subordinates that the Germans were using the monastery as an artillery observation post and had heavy weapons stored inside it. He thus wholeheartedly opposed this act of vandalism and it is a fact, proved over and over again, that on the evening before February 15 the only soldiers anywhere near the monastery were three military policemen stationed there to keep the troops out.

Freyberg appealed to Alexander, who finally agreed with him, perhaps on the evidence of a misinterpreted radio message. A German voice had been heard asking:

"'Wo ist der Abt? Ist er noch im Kloster?' (Where is the 'Abt'? Is it still in the monastery?)

"'Abt' is the German military abbreviation for 'abteilung', meaning a section. But unfortunately 'Abt' also means 'Abbot', and since 'Abt' is masculine and 'abteilung' feminine, the conversation referred to the Abbot."

Sir Henry Maitland Wilson, C.-in-C. Mediterranean, made available the necessary air formations. In the morning of February 15, therefore, 142 four-engined and 87 two-engined American bombers flew over Monte Cassino in three waves, dropping 453 tons of high explosive and incendiary bombs, and reduced the monastery of Saint Benedict to a complete and absolute ruin.

"The monks had no idea that the rumble of heavy bombers which they could hear approaching from the north concerned them in any way. Prayers were just being said in the bishop's small room. The monks were praying to the Mother of God to protect them, and when they reached the words *'pro nobis Christum exora'*, a terrific explosion shattered the peace. The first bombs were bursting. It was nine forty-five."

This bombardment, of which he disapproved, aroused two different impressions in General Clark. In his book *Calculated Risk* he says:

". . . and when the clock got around to nine-thirty, I immediately heard the first hum of engines coming up from the south. I tried to judge their progress by the steadily increasing volume of sound, a mental chore that was interrupted by a sudden roaring explosion. Sixteen bombs had been released by mistake from the American planes; several of them hit near my command post, sending fragments flying all over the place, but fortunately injuring no one, except the feelings of my police dog, Mike, who at that time was the proud mother of six week-old pups.

"Then the four groups of stately Flying Fortresses passed directly overhead and a few moments later released their bombs on Monastery Hill. I had seen the famous old Abbey, with its priceless and irreplaceable works of art, only from a distance, but with the thundering salvoes that tore apart the hillside that morning, I knew there was no possibility that I ever would see it at any closer range."

The Germans take over the monastery

But following this bombardment the German defenders moved into the ruins of the monastery and drove off with heavy losses the 4th Indian Division (Major-General Tuker) coming up to assault the peak. The 2nd New Zealand Division (Major-General Kippenberger) suffered the same fate before Cassino.

The second battle for the Liri valley was a definite success for the defenders, XIV Panzer Corps. The third brought General von Senger und Etterlin the high honour of Oak Leaves to his Iron Cross.

Clark and Freyberg, in spite of Juin's further representations in favour of the Atina manoeuvre, stuck to the narrower

pincer, which had just failed, combined with carpet bombing, which was of more use to the defenders than the attacking forces.

On March 15 775 bombers and fighter-bombers, including 260 B-17 Flying Fortresses, dropped 1,250 tons of bombs on the little town of Cassino and its immediate surroundings. It was then shelled for two hours from 1230 hours by 746 guns. But when the Ghurkas and the New Zealanders moved in to attack they found to their cost that, as Böhmler says:

"The U.S. Air Force had presented the Germans with a first-class obstacle: the towering piles of rubble, the torn and debris-strewn streets, the innumerable deep bomb craters made it quite impossible for the New Zealand 4th Armoured Brigade to penetrate into the town and support the infantry. Its tanks had to halt on the edge and leave the infantry to its own devices as soon as the latter penetrated the zone of ruin and rubble. The most strenuous efforts to clear a way for the tanks with bulldozers made painfully slow progress."

The attackers, whether stumbling over the rubble in the little town of Cassino or trying to scale the heights of the monastery above it, were up against the 1st Parachute Division, an élite German unit with a fine commander, Lieutenant-General Richard Heidrich, and commanding positions. The area was larded with mines, on one of which Major-General Kippenberger, commanding the 2nd New Zealand Division, had both his feet blown off. The defenders, though cruelly decimated, were ably supported by concentrated fire from a regiment of *Nebelwerfers*.

The fighting in the streets of Cassino resembled that in Stalingrad in its ferocity. On the slopes up to the monastery Ghurkas and paratroops fought for a few yards of ground as in the trench warfare of World War I.

On March 23 Freyberg called off his attack, which had already cost him over 2,000 men and had reached none of its objectives.

From January 16 to March 31 the American 5th Army alone suffered casualties amounting to 52,130 killed, wounded and missing (American 22,219, British 22,092, French 7,421, and Italian 398).

This would appear to justify Clausewitz's principle, quoted shortly before by Manstein to Hitler, that defence is the "most powerful form of warfare".

◁ ◁ *German officers help the abbot into the car taking him to safety.*
▽ ◁ ◁ *Cassino town after the raid of March 15, when 775 aircraft dropped 1,250 tons of bombs.*
◁ *American infantry advance along a path (marked with white tapes) cleared of mines and booby traps by the engineers.*
▽ *The monastery.*

CHAPTER III
Drive to Rome

Faced with the setbacks of Anzio and Cassino, Sir Harold Alexander now had to remedy the situation. He did so by bringing the British V Corps directly under his command and allotting to it the Adriatic sector. The British 8th Army, under the command of General Sir Oliver Leese since December 23, was given the sector between the Abruzzi peaks and the Liri valley. The American 5th Army, though still responsible for the Anzio front, was thus restricted to the area between the Liri and the Tyrrhenian Sea. It also had to hand the British X Corps, on the Garigliano, over to the 8th Army.

The decision of the Combined Chiefs-of-Staff Committee not to go on with Operation "Anvil" as the prelude to a landing in Normandy was communicated to General Maitland Wilson on February 26. He was thus able to divert to the 15th Army Group units and *matériel* previously reserved for this operation. On May 11 Alexander had under his command nine corps, of 26 divisions and about ten independent brigades.

His aim was the destruction of the German 10th Army by a double pincer movement: the first would open up the Liri valley to the Allies and the second would begin, once they had passed Frosinone, by VI Corps breaking out of the Anzio beach-head and advancing to meet them.

Juin proposes an entirely new plan

In the French Expeditionary Corps, which had taken over from the British X Corps in the Garigliano bridgehead, General Juin was not satisfied with the objective assigned to him, Monte Majo. It was the same kind of narrow turning movement "within rifle range" that had led to the Belvedere butchery and the setbacks at Cassino. So on April 4 he set out his ideas on the manoeuvre in a memorandum to General Clark. In his opinion, instead of turning right as soon as Monte Majo had been captured, "they should infiltrate under cover of surprise into the massif dominated by the Petrella and seize the

◁◁ *A cheerful column of American infantry presses on unopposed in the final swift drive on Rome.*
△ *A Canadian prepares to lob a grenade into a house suspected of containing a German position. Behind him two other Canadians are ready to rush in and mop up.*
◁ *Germans taken prisoner at Cisterna.*

key points . . . and, from there, by an outflanking movement, open the way to frontal advances mounted concurrently to secure Highway 7 and the road from Esperia up to and including the road running parallel to the front of Arce.

"The aim being to bring to bear on the Arce sector a force of considerable size so as to be able to break out in strength behind the enemy's rear and advance towards Rome."

Clark agrees

After a little hesitation Clark was won over to his subordinate's plan. This had the great advantage of including in the French Expeditionary Corps' outflanking movement the Hitler Line or "Senger defile", which blocked off the Liri valley at Pontecorvo. On the other hand there was a formidable obstacle in the Monti Aurunci, which reached over 5,000 feet at Monte Petrella. It might be assumed that the enemy had not occupied the heights in strength, and that surprise could be achieved by using the natural features as Guderian had done in the Ardennes in May 1940 and List in the Strumitsa gap on April 6, 1941.

However, everything depended on the speed with which an early success could be exploited. As usual, Kesselring would

◁ Typical Italian terrain: a constant succession of steep ridges divided by swift-flowing streams and rivers. In the foreground two Americans provide covering machine gun fire for an attack.

▽ Lieutenant-General Mark Clark, commander of the American 5th Army. Was he right to push on to the political objective of Rome rather than pursuing the military objective of cutting off major German units just north of Cassino?

△ *General Juin (centre, with goggles) explains his plans to General de Gaulle.*

▽ *French troops enter Castel Forte.*

not take long to muster his forces, but General Juin was relying on the legs of his Moroccan mountain troops and of his 4,000 mules.

Though Clark agreed to the French plan, he could not get Sir Oliver Leese to accept its corollary, the Atina plan, and though he used a corps against Cassino where Freyberg had sent in one division, the pincer was still too short and there were heavy losses.

Kesselring had 23 divisions, but most of them were worn out and short of ammunition, whereas the Allies had an abundance of everything. Here again the Germans were waging "a poor man's war" as General Westphal put it.

Another serious disadvantage for Kesselring was his enemy's overwhelming superiority in the air and at sea. This was so important that it caused him to worry not only about a landing at Civitavecchia or at Leghorn but also about whether Allied air power would cut off XIV Panzer Corps' communications at Frosinone. The uncertainty of his situation compelled Kesselring to write in his memoirs about his main reason for concern at this time: "The great dangerous unknown quantity which lasted until D-day plus 4 was the following: where would the French Expeditionary Corps be engaged, what would be its main line of advance and its composition?"

Twelve Allied v. six German divisions

And so the 10th Army and subordinate staffs were ordered to signal back with maximum urgency to Army Group as soon as the French had been identified on the front. The Expeditionary Corps had camouflaged itself so well when it moved into position in the foothills of the Monti Aurunci that Kesselring only realised it was there when the Monte Majo action was over. A clever decoy movement by Alexander made him think that the frontal attack would be combined with a landing in the area of Civitavecchia and would start on May 14.

At zero on D-day the German 10th Army was deployed as follows:

1. from the Tyrrhenian Sea to the Liri: XIV Panzer Corps (94th and 71st Infantry Divisions);
2. from the Liri to the Meta (7,400 feet): LI Mountain Corps (*Gruppe* "Baade", 1st Parachute, 44th Infantry, and 5th *Gebirgsjäger* Divisions);
3. from the Meta to the Adriatic: *Gruppe* "Hauck" (305th and 334th Infantry Divisions, 114th *Jäger* Division); and
4. in army reserve: 15th *Panzergrenadier* Division behind LI Mountain Corps.

The first encounter was thus to be

between the 12 Allied divisions (two Polish, four British, four French, and two American) and six German. The inferiority was not only numerical: at the moment when the attack started both General von Senger und Etterlin, commander of XIV Panzer Corps and Colonel-General von Vietinghoff were on leave, and, in spite of Kesselring's order, 94th Division (Lieutenant-General Steinmetz) had no men on the Petrella massif.

The French go in

At 2300 hours on May 11, 600 Allied batteries (2,400 guns ranging from 25-pounders to 9.4-inch) opened up simultaneously on a front of some 25 miles. At midnight the Allied infantry moved forward. When dawn broke both General Leese and General Clark had to admit that in spite of the surprise effect the night attack had not brought the expected success. The Polish II Corps (General Wladislas Anders: 3rd "Kressowa" and 5th "Carpathian" Divisions) had failed on the slopes of Monte Cassino and, for all the fighting spirit shown by these men, escapees from Russian jails, their losses were very heavy. In the Liri valley the British XIII Corps (Lieutenant-General Kirkman) had got two of its divisions across the Rapido, but without really denting the resistance put up by LI Mountain Corps (General Feuerstein) and here again 1st Parachute Division was particularly successful.

Though the French Expeditionary Corps had been strengthened by the 4th Moroccan Mountain Division (General Sévez) and the 1st Motorised Infantry Division (General Brosset) its task was not made any easier by the fact that the enemy opposite (71st Division: Lieutenant-General Raapke) was ready and expecting to be attacked. During this night operation, which they were ordered to carry out so as to facilitate the British XIII Corps' crossing of the Rapido, the French stumbled on to minefields and were attacked by flame-throwers. By the end of the day on the 12th it was feared that the

△ *General Anders, whose Polish troops were responsible for the final success at Cassino.*

▽ *French troops with their German prisoners at Castel Forte.*

French attack might have run out of steam and that Kesselring would have time to occupy the whole of the Petrella massif. Without losing a minute, General Juin reshaped his artillery attack so as to concentrate everything on the Monte Majo bastion. This bold stroke broke the resistance of the German 71st Division and in the afternoon of May 13 the Moroccan 2nd Division raised an immense tricolour on the top of the 3,000-foot hill. On its right the 1st Moroccan Motorised Infantry Division had cleared out the bend in the Garigliano. On its left the 3rd Algerian Division had captured Castelforte and was moving forward towards Ausonia.

The French push round the east flank

Further over to the left the American II Corps was well on its way to Formia. On that day, as Marshal Juin wrote, "having toured the fronts in the lower areas from end to end of the bridgehead where the actions were developed, I was able to see with what ardour and enthusiasm the troops drove forward to their objectives. It is true that the commanders were there in the breach in person: Brosset, driving his own jeep, was giving orders through a loud-hailer and Montsabert was conducting his battle by means of a portable radio which never left his side. There were also other reasons for this feverish excitement. Towards mid-day a message was heard in clear from the enemy ordering his troops to withdraw and the prisoners were flowing in."

Without losing a moment General Juin threw his Mountain Corps into the breach. This now included the 4th Moroccan Mountain Division and General Guillaume's Moroccan *Tabors*. Leaving the beaten tracks, with their machine guns and mortars on their backs, they scaled the steep slopes of Monte Petrella like mountain goats, reaching the top on May 15. Without waiting to get their breath back they then hurled themselves at the Revole massif (4,150 feet). Meanwhile, passing behind the Mountain Corps, the 3rd Algerian Division took Ausonia and reached Esperia, thus extending the action of the 1st Moroccan Motorised Infantry Division which had captured San Giorgio on the right bank of the Liri.

∇ The Liri valley, before Cassino. In the foreground is a knocked-out Sherman tank, and in the background an ambulance, with its crew going to pick up casualties.
▷ A road on the way to Rome under German shellfire.
∇▷ The legs of the swift Allied advance once the obstacle of Cassino had been removed.

Poles, British, and Americans drive forward

What would have happened if at the same time the British 8th Army, in a sweep as wide as General Juin had wanted, had outflanked the Pontecorvo position? In all evidence XIV Panzer Corps would have faced total disaster, a disaster which would then have overtaken the 10th Army. It was only on May 17 that the Polish II Corps, now attacking again, found the monastery on Monte Cassino deserted. It was again only on May 19 that the British 78th Division (XIII Corps) attacked the "Senger defile" in the Aquino area, but unsuccessfully. This lack of liaison between the French and the British naturally held up the French Expeditionary Corps' exploitation towards Pico and the Monti Ausoni.

But Kesselring, throwing in everything he could lay hands on, sent units of the 90th *Panzergrenadier,* the 305th, and the 26th Panzer Divisions to stop them. He also sent the 29th *Panzergrenadier* Division against the American II Corps, which had advanced through Formia and Itri and by May 22 was threatening Terracina. This was trying to pay Paul by robbing Peter, that is to say Colonel-General von Mackensen. Reinforced to the equivalent of eight divisions by the transfer of the American 36th Division to the Anzio bridgehead, the American VI Corps had no particular difficulty in breaking the resistance of the German 14th Army during the day of May 23. Forty-eight hours later II and VI Corps met on the shores of Lake Fogliano. On the same May 23 the French Expeditionary Corps was spreading out over the Monti Ausoni whilst the Canadian I Corps (Lieutenant-General E. L. M. Burns: 1st Infantry and 5th Armoured Divisions), which had just relieved the British XIII Corps, was forcing its way through the Pontecorvo defile.

Kesselring attempts to cover Rome

Kesselring tried once more to protect Rome by establishing a new position on the line Colli Laziali–Monti Lepini to secure Vietinghoff's right, and to achieve this he withdrew from the Leghorn area his last reserve motorised division, the "Hermann Göring" Panzer Division, and sent it immediately to Valmontone. The bombing by the Anglo-American air force, which on one single day (May 26) destroyed 665 vehicles of the 14th Army alone, considerably held up these troop movements. Now Valmontone was, in accordance with General Alexander's instructions, precisely the objective of the American VI Corps. If Truscott, now in Cisterna, therefore advanced with the main body of his forces along the Corti–Artena axis, he had every chance of cutting off the 10th Army's move to cover Rome. The latter's rearguard was still at Ceprano, some 40 miles or more from Valmontone, and the Germans would thus be driven back against the Abruzzi mountains, which were virtually impassable, and entirely cut off.

But, for reasons which Alexander said were inexplicable, Clark ordered VI Corps to attack with its 34th, 45th Infantry, and 1st Armoured Divisions north west to the line Velletri–Colli Laziali, sending only a slightly reinforced 3rd Division along the Valmontone axis (northwards). This decision, taken in the afternoon of May 25, brought only a slight reaction from Alexander, who remarked to General Gruenther, the American 5th Army chief-of-staff, when the latter brought him the news: "I am sure that the army commander will continue to push toward Valmontone, won't he?"

"Rome the great prize" was the title General Mark Clark gave to the 15th chapter of his memoirs. We are thus forced to conclude that this able but impetuous man had lost sight of the fact that a commander's supreme reward is to receive in his tent those who have been sent on behalf of the enemy commander to sue for conditions of surrender. But Alexander was also taken in by the Roman mirage at this time: did he not forbid the French Expeditionary Corps, then coming down from the Monti Lepini,

◁◁ *Homeless Italians strive to escape from the war.*
▽ ◁◁ *Italian refugees pass through the Allied lines on their way to the safety of rear areas.*
◁ *A village destroyed in the Allied advance from Cassino.*
▽ *Clark (left) enters the suburbs of Rome.*
Overleaf: *Rome was the first Axis capital to fall to the Allies, and in a special ceremony in July, the American flag that had been flying over the White House on December 7, 1941 was raised in front of the Victor Emmanuel II monument. The troops taking part in the retreat ceremony were found by the 85th Division.*

to use the Frosinone–Rome highway, which he intended to restrict to the British 8th Army?

Oddly enough, back in London, Churchill tried to put Alexander on his guard against the attractions of this prestige objective. On May 28 he wrote to him: "at this distance it seems much more important to cut their line of retreat than anything else. I am sure you will have carefully considered moving more armour by the Appian Way up to the northernmost spearhead directed against the Valmontone-Frosinone road. A cop is much more important than Rome which would anyhow come as its consequence. The cop is the one thing that matters." Two days later he came back to the point: "But I should feel myself wanting in comradeship if I did not let you know that the glory of this battle, already great, will be measured, not by the capture of Rome or the juncture with the bridgehead, but by the number of German divisions cut off. I am sure you will have revolved all this in your mind, and perhaps you have already acted in this way. Nevertheless I feel I ought to tell you that it is the cop that counts."

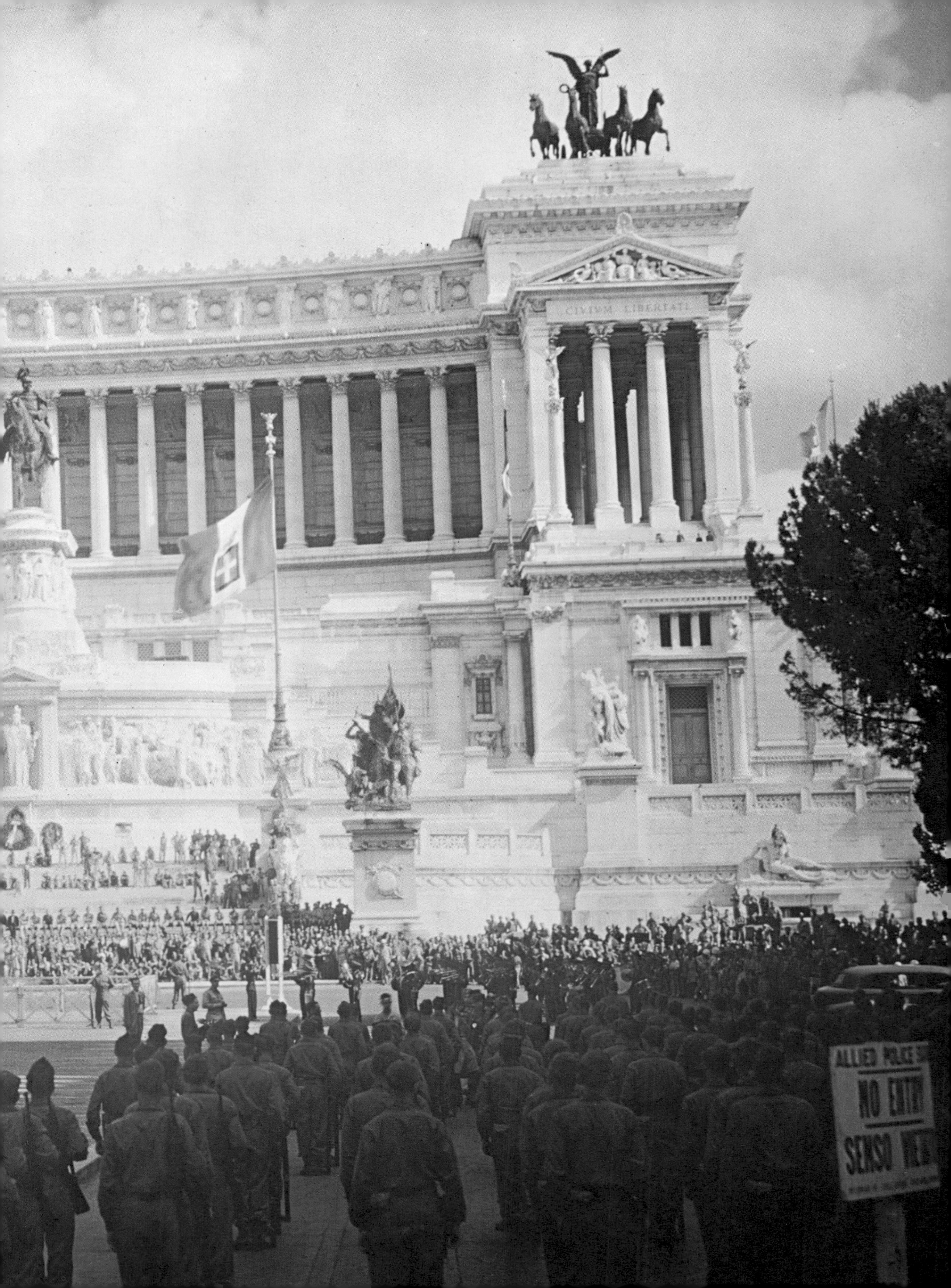
CIVIVM LIBERTATI
ALLIED POLICE
NO ENTRY
SENSO

▷ *A happy group of Italians watches flour supplies for the bakeries of Rome being unloaded. Within a few days of Rome's capture, the Allies were feeding about 500,000 of the city's population.*
▽ *Men of the Italian Co-Belligerent Forces, newly supplied with British equipment, parade through Rome.*
▷▷ *American troops in Victor Emmanuel II Square.*
▽▷▷ *A 5th Army patrol in Rome.*

Rome declared an "open city"

These were words of wisdom indeed, but in Italy the die was cast in the shape of the objective given to the American VI Corps. On May 31 its 36th Division found a gap in the German 14th Army defences, turned the Velletri position and scaled the Colli Laziali. Furious at this setback, Kesselring recalled Mackensen and replaced him by General Lemelsen. He now had to order the evacuation of Rome, which he proclaimed an "open city". On June 4 the American 88th Division (Major-General J. E. Sloan) was the first unit to enter the Eternal City.

General Clark tells a story worthy of inclusion in any history of the campaign. Writing of his first visit to Rome he says:

"Many Romans seemed to be on the

verge of hysteria in their enthusiasm for the American troops. The Americans were enthusiastic too, and kept looking for ancient landmarks that they had read about in their history books. It was on that day that a doughboy made the classic remark of the Italian campaign when he took a long look at the ruins of the old Colosseum, whistled softly, and said, 'Geez, I didn't know our bombers had done *that* much damage in Rome!'"

German and Allied losses

On May 11 Kesselring had 23 divisions. These had been reduced to remnants. The 44th, 71st, 94th, 362nd, and 715th had been virtually wiped out. His Panzer and *Panzergrenadier* divisions had lost most of their equipment. Amongst the reinforcements which Hitler had sent

through the Brenner there were badly trained divisions such as the 162nd, recruited from Turkman contingents, the Luftwaffe 20th Infantry Division, and the 16th *Panzergrenadier* Division of the *Waffen* S.S. These went to pieces at the first onslaught.

During the same period the Americans lost 18,000 killed, missing, and wounded, the British 10,500, the French 7,260, the Canadians 3,742, and the Poles 3,700. Some 25,000 Allied prisoners were taken.

These losses were not enough to holc up the 15th Army Group's advance Also, in North Africa the 9th Colonia Infantry Division and the 1st and 5tl French Armoured Divisions were now ready for combat. It is clear that a bolc action along the Rome–Terni–Ancona axis could have brought to an end al enemy resistance south of the Apennines

Churchill wrote to Alexander on May 31: "I will support you in obtaining the firs priority in everything you need to achiev

▽ *Mark Clark talks to a priest outside St. Peter's on his arrival in the city on June 4.*

this glorious victory. I am sure the American Chiefs of Staff would now feel this was a bad moment to pull out of the battle or in any way weaken its force for the sake of other operations of an amphibious character, which may very soon take their place in the van of our ideas."

In other words the Prime Minister was flattering himself that he could get General Marshall to abandon Operation "Anvil" and exploit the victories of the 15th Army Group across the Apennines towards the Tarvis col, then on through the Ljubljana gap, with Vienna as the final objective. A grandiose plan, no doubt, but possible on May 31. It would have been even more possible if, as he put it, the German 10th and 14th Armies had been "copped" south of Rome as originally suggested.

Churchill's position *vis-à-vis* Marshall would clearly have been stronger had General Alexander shown more authority in his relationship with Clark and if he

▽ *American troops celebrate the fall of Rome.*

△ *Lieutenant Rex Metcalfe of Flint, Michigan, inspects his men before setting off to do guard duty.*

had given the British 8th Army's operations the direction and the scope that General Juin had recommended at the time of Cassino.

It has been repeatedly said that Marshall, imposing as he did on his rather unwilling colleagues the literal execution of the inter-Allied decisions taken at Teheran, was making himself Roosevelt's spokesman to Churchill and Sir Alan Brooke, for the President was anxious not to get Allied armies embroiled in the Danube basin, the private preserve of Stalin. This would seem to betray an ignorance of the nature of the relationships between the White House and the Pentagon.

Unlike Churchill, Roosevelt intervened very little in the conduct of operations unless there was disagreement between the American war leaders and he had to impose his authority as President. The categorical refusal of the Americans to agree to the British request for a revision of the overall inter-Allied strategy must therefore be attributed mainly to General Marshall. Marshall, we believe, was only obeying the dictates of high strategy. It was clear to him, in effect, that an Anglo-American drive towards Vienna, and out of line with the main thrust, would contribute less to the success of Operation "Overlord" than would a landing in Provence, which would open up the ports of Marseilles and Toulon to Allied men and *matériel,* whilst a strong Franco-American force, operating first up the Rhône, then the Saône, would give a right wing to Eisenhower when he broke out into Champagne. To him this reasoning respected the principle of the convergence of effort, so dear to American military doctrine. It can easily be seen how Marshall froze at Churchill's passionate arguments.

Kesselring re-establishes himself in the Apennines

Although Roosevelt could not accept his colleague's views, he was nevertheless unable to bring nearer by even a single day because of questions of transport, men, and *matériel,* the start of Operation "Anvil" scheduled for August 15. Between June 11 and July 22, three American and five French divisions successively dropped out and became inactive, though the 9th Colonial Division did take Elba between July 17 and 19 in Operation "Brassard", led by General de Lattre de Tassigny. This Allied inactivity allowed Kesselring, who lost no chances, to re-establish himself in the Apennines and especially to give Field-Marshal von Rundstedt his 3rd and 15th *Panzergrenadier* Divisions, whilst the "Hermann Göring" Panzer Division was sent off to the Eastern Front.

As for the case for getting to the Danube basin before the Russians, Marshall was not qualified to follow the Prime Minister in this field, which was reserved for politicians. It will be noticed that less than a year later General Eisenhower adopted the same attitude when, having reached the Elbe, he showed little further interest in Berlin which, from the strictly military point of view, was no longer of any importance.